QUICK
REFERENCE
ENCYCLOPEDIA

DREW KNOWLES

SANTA
MONICA
PRESS

Copyright © 2008 by Drew Knowles

Published by:

Santa Monica Press LLC
P.O. Box 1076
Santa Monica, CA 90406-1076
1-800-784-9553
www.santamonicapress.com
books@santamonicapress.com

Printed in the United States

Santa Monica Press books are available at special quantity discounts when purchased in bulk by corporations, organizations, or groups. Please call our Special Sales department at 1-800-784-9553.

ISBN-13 978-1-59580-034-3
ISBN-10 1-59580-034-4

Library of Congress Cataloging-in-Publication Data

Knowles, Drew, 1956–
  Route 66 quick reference encyclopedia / by Drew Knowles.
     p. cm.
  ISBN-13: 978-1-59580-034-3
  ISBN-10: 1-59580-034-4
  1. United States Highway 66--Encyclopedias. 2. United States Highway 66--History--Encyclopedias. 3. Roads--United States--History--Encyclopedias. 4. United States--Description and travel--Encyclopedias. 5. United States--History, Local--Encyclopedias. 6. Automobile travel--United States--Encyclopedias. 7. Historic sites--United States--Encyclopedias. 8. Roadside architecture--United States--Encyclopedias. 9. United States Highway 66--Maps. I. Title.
  HE356.U55K58 2008
  917.804'34--dc22
                              2008001802

Cover and interior design and production by Future Studio

Contents

Acknowledgments

I t's true that no writer goes it alone. I want to take this opportunity to thank some of the people who contributed— some directly, some indirectly—to the completion of this *Quick Reference*. But before I do, let me acknowledge that any errors or omissions rest entirely with me.

Whether for sharing their personal experience and expertise, or for providing their generous support and encouragement of my own humble contributions to the Route 66 renaissance, the following people deserve special thanks: Kathy Anderson, David Clark and Carol Krohn, Marian Clark, Jim Conkle, Linda and Rocky Drake, Carol Duncan, Denny Gibson, Shellee Graham, Lucille Hamons, Michele Hansford, Dan and Sheila Harlow, Carolyn Hasenfratz, Debra Hodkin, Fran Houser, Bill Kaszynski, Susan Croce Kelly, Gerald Knowles, David and Mary Lou Knudson, Geoff Ladd, Bob and Ramona Lehman, Croc and Cheryl Lile, Jerry McClanahan, Jeff Meyer, Terrence Moore, Ralph Oliver, Scott Piotrowski, Sue Preston, Emily Priddy, Wanda Queenan, Becky Ransom, James Rosin, Jim Ross, Bill Shea, Pat Smith,

Michael Taylor, Tom Teague, Delbert and Ruth Trew, Bob Waldmire, Sue Waldmire, Michael and Suzanne Wallis, Mike Ward, Ron Warnick, Dawn Welch, Terry Wrinkle, and Fred Zander.

And finally, thanks to my wife Lauren for being the world's best traveling companion.

Foreword

by Susan Croce Kelly

Author of

Route 66: The Highway and Its People

The first intrepid travelers along Route 66 in the 1920s had to bring their own tents, not to mention automobile repair equipment and frying pans. Signage along the road in those early days was iffy, and pavement was almost nonexistent.

Today, Route 66 pilgrims can count on pavement and places to eat, sleep and get their cars fixed. But information can still be hard to come by. Modern Route 66 explorers may, in some cases, be looking for a particular stretch of the earliest highway route. That's a very tough question. But they may have other kinds of questions, too, things like: "Where is the Wigwam Motel?" "When was 'Get Your Kicks on Route 66' written and who was the singer who made it famous?" "Is there any connection between the wonderful old movie theatres in Miami, Oklahoma, and Gallup, New Mexico?" "Who named it 'The Mother Road'?"

Drew Knowles has spent years traveling Route 66, and like so many other travelers, he had questions of his own. Happily for us, Knowles not only hunted down answers to his questions but he decided to share them. This *Route 66 Quick Reference Encyclopedia* is an invaluable tool for both the casual traveler and the serious student of The World That Is Route 66. And while the 400 entries won't answer every question a person may have about Route 66— no book could—it is a good starting place.

The following pages are full of nuggets of history, pop culture, geography and even highway technology, not to mention a variety of maps. It's the kind of book that should be part of every trip down Route 66, whether the trip is by car or by imagination.

Author's Preface

I've been exploring, photographing, and otherwise enjoying Route 66—and the people who make it what it is—for over 15 years now. During that time, I've talked with a large number of people who know a great deal about Route 66, and I've tried to walk away from each of those encounters just a little more informed.

The bare bones of the facts, factoids, and minutiae I've picked up during those 15 years are contained in this *Quick Reference.* Sometimes I feel like a slow learner, because I can't help but think that it really shouldn't take 15 years to learn what I've learned.

And that's why this book exists: so that everyone else who's curious enough to want to know more about America's most famous highway can find out *what* they want, *when* they want, quickly and easily.

And there's something I've learned that can't be found in the hundreds of definitions and descriptions assembled here—something each of us finds out on our own. And that's the realization that the scholars, historians, business people, and other denizens of Route 66 are some of the kindest, most generous, most gracious people on Earth.

So, after digesting some of this little book, I hope you'll be inspired to hop in your car, take a drive on Route 66, and find out for yourself what all the fuss is about. There really is no substitute for your own experience.

—Drew Knowles
Fort Worth, Texas

A Short Introduction to

ROUTE 66

I t comes as a surprise to many people that Route 66, rather than being the product of a grand construction project, was actually cobbled together from parts already on hand.

Native Americans, long before European colonizers arrived on the scene, crisscrossed parts of North America with hunting trails and trade routes that were typically no more than footpaths. These were later widened and experienced greater use as the colonial population expanded.

In the eighteenth and nineteenth centuries, there were efforts at local levels to improve existing trails and to create new ones for purposes of improved commerce. But even so, they were unpaved and primitive as a rule, which meant that they were nearly unusable in severe weather. The proliferation of railroad lines during this period served to make the poor condition of roads less important than it otherwise would have been.

Starting around 1890, there was a

surge in interest in bicycling, and bicycles were soon joined by the earliest automobiles. Proponents of these voguish conveyances began to clamor for more and better roads on which to operate them, resulting in the Good Roads Movement.

The early decades of the twentieth century saw the development of a significant number of "named" auto trails, such as the Lincoln Highway and Ozark Trail. As in the past, these were funded and otherwise furthered at the local and regional levels. Signposts, trees, and other objects became covered with a multitude of symbols, one for each of the trails any given roadway might be considered a part of. Early motorists might have to stop and gaze for some time at this extensive "menu" of routes before deciding in which direction to proceed.

It was into this highway environment that the federal government thrust itself in the 1920s. In order to bring some order to the chaos and cacophony, the Joint Board on Interstate Highways and the American Association of State Highway Officials in 1926 enacted the numbering system for interstate highways with which we are familiar and of which U.S. 66 was a part.

It didn't happen overnight of course, but over the next several years the confusing riot of named trail placards was replaced by black-and-white numbered shields of standardized appearance. Even numbers signified east-west routes, while odd numbers designated north-south routes. Numbers ending in zero were reserved for coast-to-coast highways.

In each case, though—including 66 —these numbered routes were established simply through the placement of numbered navigational signs at key points along pre-existing roads, and there was considerable competition among affected towns and cities to have these newly designated routes pass through their communities on their streets. While there was certainly a bias for paved, or "improved" roads, in many areas there was no paved option available in 1926. It was not until the late 1930s that the whole length of Route 66 was a paved surface.

U.S. 66 underwent considerable change and improvement during the 1930s, as American highways in general were beneficiaries of Depression-era initiatives such as the Works Progress Administration (WPA) and the Civilian Conservation Corps (CCC). Then, during World War II, civilian travel diminished sharply with the rationing of tires and fuel. Those years, however, constituted the "calm before the storm."

It was a scant 10-year period following the end of the war for which Route 66 became best known. It was from roughly 1946 to 1955 that the highway sustained its heaviest usage, becoming a main artery for Americans spending leisure time on vacations and, in many cases, moving permanently to the western part of the country.

In 1956, the U.S. Congress passed the National Interstate and Defense Highways Act, which called for the construction of a nationwide network of high-speed, limited-access highways modeled in part after the German autobahns. As construction of these "interstates" progressed, portions of Route 66 (and the other old highways) were bypassed and fell into disuse. Businesses—and the people whose livelihoods depended on the steady flow of traffic Route 66 had provided—began to suffer. Untold numbers of those businesses ceased operation.

It was not until 1985 that the bypassing of Route 66 by the interstates was completed. In that year, the last segment in Williams, Arizona, was replaced by a just-completed section of Interstate 40, and U.S. Route 66 passed into history.

Along much of its length, the old highway was cast aside with little thought—essentially ignored—and is still there for today's explorer to find and experience. However, the condition of the road and its associated structures is in many places deplorable, which has led to the establishment of a number of preservation-oriented organizations whose objective is to save what remains of Route 66 for future generations.

Thanks in part to those efforts, today—more than 20 years after U.S. 66 supposedly took its last breath—you can still get a taste of what the interstates thoughtlessly tried to take away from you.

Maps

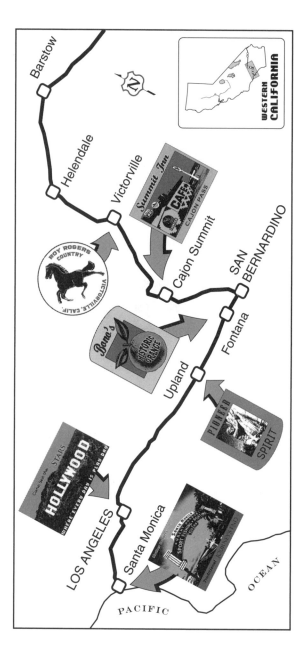

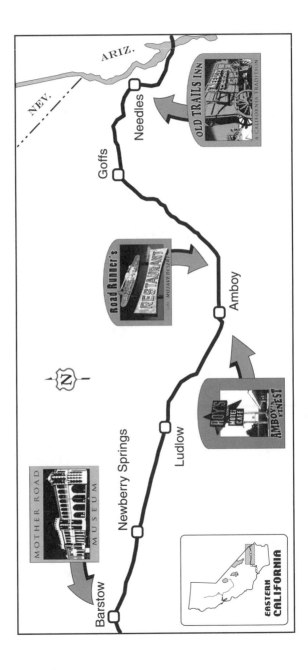

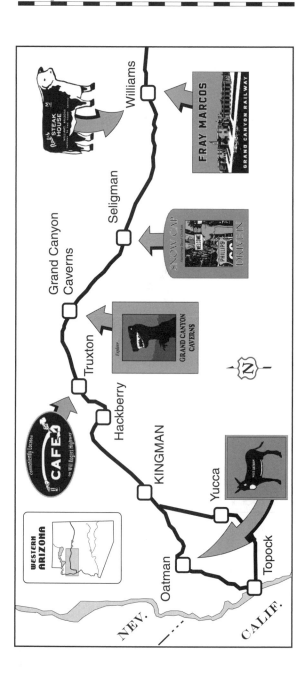

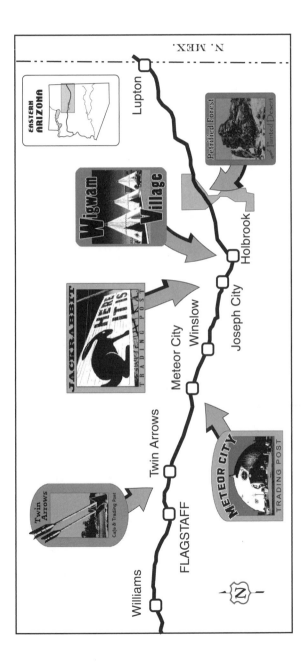

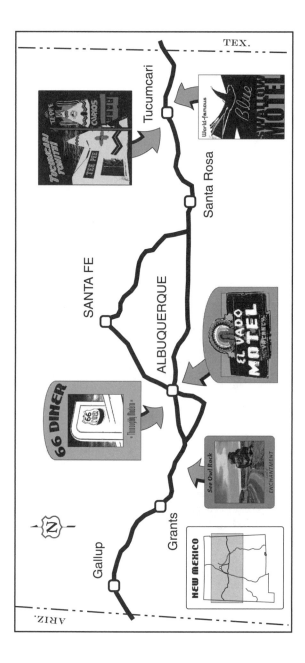

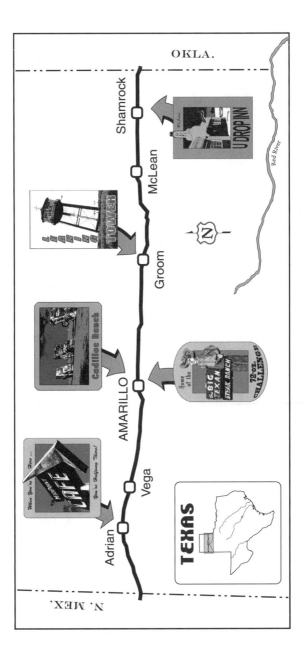

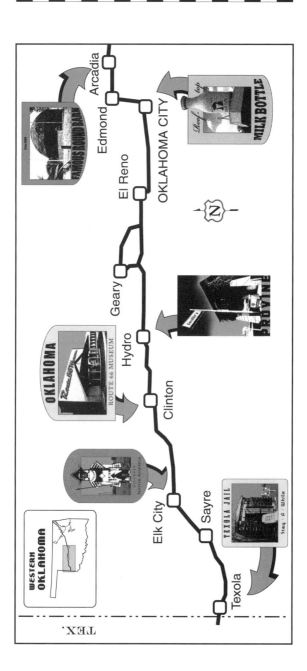

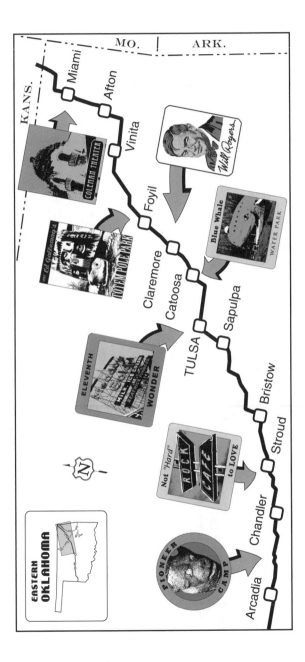

EASTERN OKLAHOMA

MO. | ARK.

KANS.

Miami
Afton
Vinita
Foyil
Claremore
Catoosa
TULSA
Sapulpa
Bristow
Stroud
Chandler
Arcadia

COLEMAN THEATER

Wild Rogers

Blue Whale WATER PARK

"El Gallinazo" TOTEM POLE PARK

ELEVENTH WONDER

Not "Hard" ROCK CAFE to LOVE

PIONEER CAMP

–N–

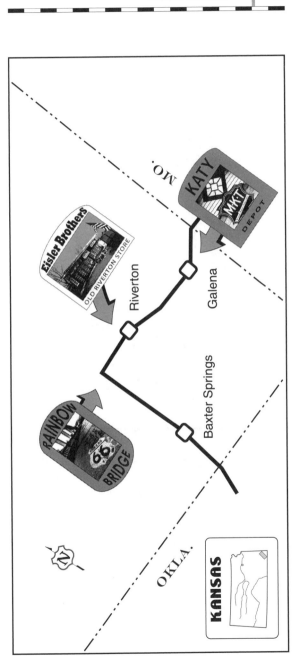

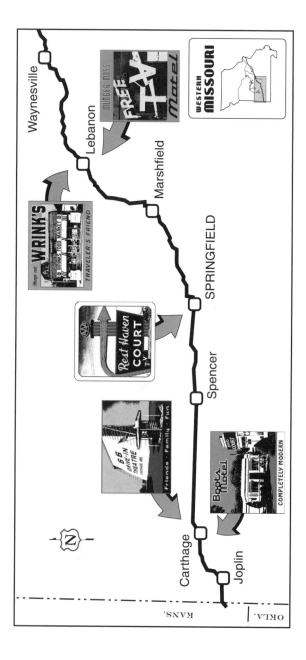

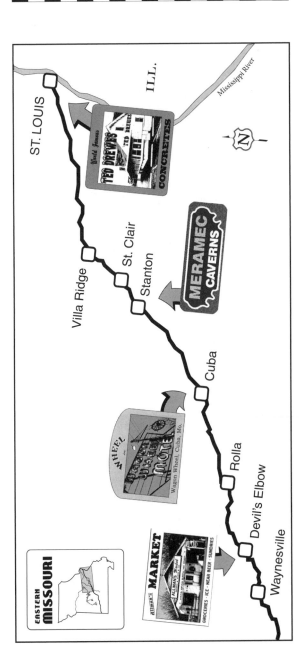

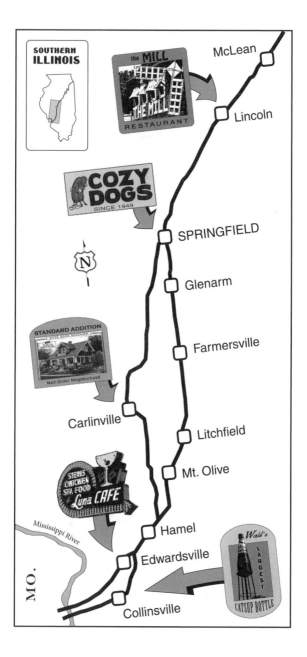

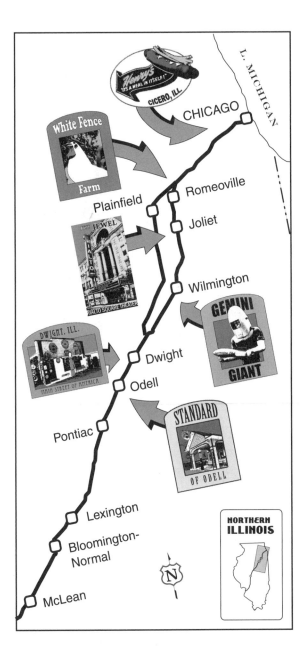

A Route 66 Timeline

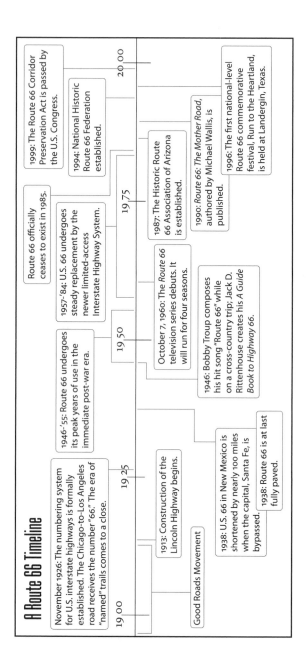

1900

Good Roads Movement

1925

November 1926: The numbering system for U.S. interstate highways is formally established. The Chicago-to-Los Angeles road receives the number "66." The era of "named" trails comes to a close.

1913: Construction of the Lincoln Highway begins.

1938: U.S. 66 in New Mexico is shortened by nearly 100 miles when the capital, Santa Fe, is bypassed.

1938: Route 66 is at last fully paved.

1950

1946–'55: Route 66 undergoes its peak years of use in the immediate post-war era.

1946: Bobby Troup composes his hit song "Route 66" while on a cross-country trip; Jack D. Rittenhouse creates his A Guide Book to Highway 66.

October 7, 1960: The Route 66 television series debuts. It will run for four seasons.

1975

Route 66 officially ceases to exist in 1985.

1957–'84: U.S. 66 undergoes steady replacement by the newer limited-access Interstate Highway System.

1987: The Historic Route 66 Association of Arizona is established.

1990: Route 66: The Mother Road, authored by Michael Wallis, is published.

2000

1999: The Route 66 Corridor Preservation Act is passed by the U.S. Congress.

1994: National Historic Route 66 Federation established.

1996: The first national-level Route 66 commemorative festival, Run to the Heartland, is held at Landergin, Texas.

100th Meridian

The 100th meridian is an imaginary line, 100 degrees west of Greenwich, which traditionally delineates the boundary between the arable east and the relatively arid west, which for the most part requires irrigation for farming. The 100th meridian today also forms Oklahoma's western border with Texas,

although at one time a portion of that border would have followed the North Fork of the Red River, which would have meant that Oklahoma towns such as Texola and Erick would have been part of Texas. There is a museum in Erick dedicated to the 100th meridian and its historical and cultural significance.

2,448

This figure is often given as the number of miles of Route 66 from Chicago to Santa Monica; however, since the highway was continually rerouted throughout its long life, there is no single official number that truly describes Route 66's length. As an example, in 1946, when Jack D. Rittenhouse drove the route and wrote his seminal postwar guide to the highway, the mileage was 2,295.

66 Bowl
(Oklahoma City, OK) A bowling alley on the west side of town (39th Expressway) with a 1950s-era sign by the highway.

66 Courts
(Groom, TX) A now-demolished motel court with an adjacent gasoline station designed with subtle Art Deco influence and clad in stucco. The 66 Courts were an inspiration in the design of one of the new rest areas on nearby Interstate 40.

66 Diner
(Albuquerque, NM) Streamline-Moderne-style diner that is also headquarters for the New Mexico Route 66 Association. The building burned in 1995, but has since been beautifully restored.

66 Drive-In Theater
(Carthage, MO) Orig-
inally opened for
business in 1949, this
drive-in theater on the
west side of town has
been nicely restored,
and grand reopening
ceremonies were held
in 1998.

89ers
A secondary nickname referring to the citizens who settled in Oklahoma at the time
of the land rushes of 1889. Since many of
these settlers moved into the area prema-
turely, they caused Oklahomans in general
to be called "Sooners" (the primary, official nickname for Oklahomans).

9-Foot
Describing the approximate width of some
old, discontinuous fragments of Route 66
in northeastern Oklahoma, sometimes referred to as the "sidewalk highway." See
also SIDEWALK HIGHWAY.

Ace in the Hole
Motion picture starring Kirk Douglas (later
rereleased under the title *The Big Carnival*)
that was filmed on location on some cliffs
beside U.S. 66 in western New Mexico,

near Manuelito, in the early 1950s.

Adopt-a-Stretch

A program administered by the National Historic Route 66 Federation, wherein individuals "adopt" 100-mile stretches of the old highway and make it a point to keep up with significant changes occurring in that segment. These individuals also contribute review material for the Dining and Lodging Guide published periodically by the Federation.

Albino Squirrels

The town of Marionville, Missouri is known for its wild albino squirrels. Far from being a myth, they are highly publicized and touted by area boosters. While Marionville is not actually on U.S. 66, it is just a few miles southwest of Springfield on U.S. 60.

Alignment

The path that a highway takes through a given area; relevant because over the years a highway's alignment may change many times, particularly its passage through cities. Typically, Route 66's early city alignments passed directly along downtown streets, which in later years made for intolerable traffic conditions, leading to the re-aligning of the highway so that it would skirt (or "bypass") the core of the city. It is also significant to note that certain areas, particularly larger cities, often had multiple official alignments in existence at the same time, affording the motorist more than one option. Aside from the primary alignment, which would carry the simple "66" designation, there might also be a "City 66" and/or "ALT 66" available. See also BYPASS.

Alvarado Hotel

(Albuquerque, NM) Harvey House hotel and dining room that was closed in 1969 and demolished in 1970. In 2002, a "new" Alvarado was completed on the site of the original, and it now functions as the city's public transit hub. See also HARVEY HOUSE.

"Amarillo's Finest"

Phrase appended to the sign for the Big 8 Motel of El Reno, Oklahoma, for its use in the filming of the 1988 feature film *Rain Man.* The motel has since been demolished. See also BIG 8 MOTEL.

Amboy

Tiny community in the desert country of

Southern California consisting of little more than a motel, restaurant, and gasoline station that once catered to Highway 66

travelers. In 2005, the entire town was purchased by entrepreneur/restaurateur Albert Okura, who promised to restore it to some semblance of its authentic past. See also ROY'S MOTEL & CAFÉ.

Amboy Crater

A volcanic cinder cone just south and west of the Route 66 town of Amboy, California. From old 66, turn south on Crater Road for a closer approach. There is also a footpath that takes you to the top of the cinder cone, but note that a hike to the top and back can take 2–3 hours.

Anasazi

A Native-American culture that flourished in the Four Corners region of the U.S. several centuries ago, from which the Pueblo peoples of today are thought to be descended. These include the Navajo, Hopi, and Zuni, all of whom occupy lands adjacent to Route 66 in northwestern New Mexico and northeastern Arizona. The region includes many examples of ancient cliff dwellings attributed to the Anasazi.

Ant Farm

Originally founded by a pair of architecture graduates in the late 1960s and active for about 10 years, this art collective at one time or another was comprised of several individuals, notably Doug Michels and Chip Lord (founders), Curtis Schreier, Hudson Marquez, and Douglas Hurr. Their best-known project was completed in 1974 and dubbed Cadillac Ranch. See also CADILLAC RANCH.

Ariston Café

(Litchfield, IL) Restaurant operating at the current location since 1935. The family originally started busi-ness in 1924 in Carlinville (prior to Route 66's establishment) but moved when 66 was rerouted and traffic patterns shifted.

ARK

Acronym for Animal Reptile Kingdom, a bygone roadside menagerie located adjacent to the Blue Whale of Catoosa. See also BLUE WHALE.

Arrowood Trading Post

(Catoosa, OK) Former trading post just across the highway from the Blue Whale of Catoosa. Also known as the Chief Wolf Robe Trading Post. See also BLUE WHALE.

Arroyo Seco

Spanish for "dry streambed," the Arroyo Seco is a watercourse that runs largely underground in the Los Angeles area. U.S. 66 roughly paralleled the Arroyo Seco, and was eventually realigned onto the Arroyo Seco Parkway once that roadway was completed circa 1940. The Arroyo Seco Parkway enjoys the distinction of being the first limited-access highway west of the Mississippi River.

Art Institute of Chicago

(Chicago, IL) Situated near the easternmost end of Route 66, the Art Institute serves as a useful landmark for beginning one's Mother Road adventure. The institute has been a training ground for numerous well-known American artists over the years, and it has a prestigious collection that includes works by such artistic luminaries as Edward Hopper, Frederic Remington, and James McNeill Whistler.

Asphalt
Technically, a naturally occurring semisolid useful as a binder and in waterproofing, similar to tar. The term is commonly used to refer to what is more properly called asphalt concrete, a mixture of asphalt and mineral aggregate that, when compacted, is used in the paving of roads. Compare with CONCRETE.

Association
See ROUTE 66 ASSOCIATIONS.

AT&SF
Atchison, Topeka and Santa Fe Railroad. This railroad's southwestern trunk closely paralleled U.S. Highway 66 in New Mexico, Arizona, and  Southern California. For today's 66 traveler, this means that many towns in the region boast fine examples of well-designed depots and hotels from the heyday of railroad travel, many of which come from the railroad's close association with Fred Harvey. See also HARVEY HOUSE.

Bob Audette

A longtime Route 66 activist, Audette was a cofounder of the Route 66 Chamber of Commerce and designer of New Mexico's Route 66 commemorative license plates. In 2006, he was the recipient of the Lifetime Achievement Award presented in Albuquerque.

Cyrus Avery

The "Father of Route 66." Avery was a Tulsa-area businessman who championed the idea of a major cross-country highway passing through his home state of Oklahoma. The road he managed to bring about was eventually designated U.S. 66 when the numbered system of highways was formally introduced in 1926.

Aztec Hotel

(Monrovia, CA) Hotel dating from 1925 that was designed with a pre-Columbian theme. It includes a row of storefronts resembling an early Meso-American temple. The hotel was undergoing an extensive restoration in 2007.

Bagdad Café

1. Café that formerly stood in the town of Bagdad, California, and which inspired the 1987 movie of the same name. The movie, however, was filmed in the nearby town of

Newberry Springs. 2. A café in Newberry Springs, California, where the film *Bagdad Café* was shot. At the time of the filming, it was called the Sidewinder Café; however, in order to take advantage of its film history, it has since changed its name to Bagdad Café.

Balanced Rock
An eroded rock formation that once stood east of Albuquerque, New Mexico, in the Tijeras Canyon area. At one time it featured a painted mural advertising Queens Rest Camp at 6200 Central Avenue. Balanced Rock was considered unstable, however, and the state highway department removed it in the early 1950s.

Beer Nuts
(Bloomington, IL) Well-known American snack-food brand with its headquarters in the Route 66 town of Bloomington. There is a gift shop on premises and visitors can view a video of the manufacturing process.

Beltline
A traffic route which skirts a city's downtown area in order to avoid traffic congestion, sometimes completely encircling the city; bypass. For a specific example, see BRITTON. See also BYPASS.

Bent Door

(Adrian, TX) A building near the midpoint of U.S. 66 that has an unusually shaped front door, said to have been salvaged from an airport observation booth. The building at one time—and may yet again—house a roadside café.

Big 8 Motel

(El Reno, OK) No longer standing, this motel achieved notoriety after having been used as a location in the 1988 film *Rain Man*, for which its exterior sign was modified to include the phrase "Amarillo's Finest." In fact, El Reno is approximately 250 miles east of Amarillo, Texas.

The Big Carnival

Alternate title for the film *Ace in the Hole*. The film, originally released in 1951, was rereleased a few years later under the new name. See also ACE IN THE HOLE.

Big Texan

(Amarillo, TX) World-famous steakhouse known for its offer of a free 72-ounce steak dinner to anyone who can eat all of it in one hour; officially Big Texan Steak Ranch. Once a Route 66 fixture, the Big Texan moved to the side of Interstate 40 circa 1968 in response to changing American travel patterns. The Big Texan's attached gift shop includes a display of live rattlesnakes, a throwback to the heyday of Route 66 when reptile farms were popular roadside attractions. [72 oz. = 2,041 g]

Biograph Theater

(Chicago, IL) Theater famous as the site of

the killing of gangster John Dillinger by law enforcement agents. The Biograph formerly stood at 2433 N. Lincoln Avenue.

Black Gumbo

A term used to describe the local soil near Jericho, Texas. See JERICHO GAP.

Blarney Stone

A particular stone in a castle in County Cork, Ireland. Legend states that the stone will confer skill in flattery or storytelling on anyone who kisses it. Elmore Park in Shamrock, Texas, contains what is reputed to be a fragment of the true Blarney Stone.

Blue Dome

(Tulsa, OK) An automotive service station on an old alignment of 66 in Tulsa distinguished by its blue-domed roofline.

Blue Hole

(Santa Rosa, NM) Said to be some 80 feet deep, this is the most famous of the many bodies of water in this vicinity suitable for skin/scuba diving. The waters of the Blue Hole are approximately 64°F (18°C) year-round.

Blue Plate

Describing a full-meal menu selection at a diner or café, typically offered at a special price, i.e., the "blue plate special." The term is thought to originate from blue-patterned dishware commonly used for serving.

Blue Swallow Motel

(Tucumcari, NM) Completed in the early 1940s, this motel was given as an engage-

ment present to Lillian Redman in 1958, who operated it for the next 40 years. The Blue Swallow is much renowned for its mid-twentieth-century authenticity, including the very large, neon-illuminated, one-of-a-kind sign. See also LILLIAN REDMAN.

Blue Whale (or Catoosa Whale)

(Catoosa, OK) A true roadside attraction of the old school, the Blue Whale of Catoosa is the centerpiece of a small 1970s-era water park.

The whale sits at the edge of a pond with several picnic tables nearby. Back in the day, Route 66 motorists in the mood for a swim could enter the whale's mouth, and from there make a splash into the pond either by diving from the whale's tail fin, or by sliding down a chute on one side. The park was closed circa 1980 and remained idle for many years. In 2002, the whale and other features of the park were refurbished by volunteers as part of the Save-A-Landmark program. See also SAVE-A-LANDMARK.

Boller Brothers

The architectural team of Carl and Robert Boller specialized in the design of American movie theaters in the Midwest and Southwest during the 1920s and 1930s. Some of their more highly regarded theater designs can be found in Route 66 towns, including the KiMo (Albuquerque, New Mexico), the Coleman (Miami, Oklahoma), and the El Morro (Gallup, New Mexico). See also KiMO; COLEMAN.

Bono's Historic Orange

(Fontana, CA) A roadside vending stand in the form of a giant orange. At one time, there were several

of these scattered in Southern California. This area was once a hub for citrus growers.

Boot Hill

Traditional name for cemeteries in the American West, especially ones in which gunfighters are buried. This stems from the expression that when one dies fighting, he has died "with his boots on." There are numerous graveyards so named, including one in Tascosa, Texas, north of U.S. 66 in Oldham County.

Boots Motel

(Carthage, MO) A vintage motel exhibit-

ing characteristics of Streamline Moderne styling and named for its founder, Arthur Boots. See also STREAMLINE MODERNE.

Bottle Tree Forest

(Oro Grande, CA) A folk-art feature constructed by Elmer Long beginning in approximately 2000, it is made from thousands of glass bottles and other detritus collected by Mr. Long from the surrounding desert and assembled into hundreds of treelike structures. It was inspired in part by a similar display of discarded bottles near Hesperia, California. That display was part of Hula Ville, which met its end in the mid-1990s. See also FOLK ART; HULA VILLE.

Bridgehead Inn

(Times Beach, MO) Former Route 66 roadhouse west of St. Louis that now serves as the headquarters and visitors' center for Route 66 State Park. See also ROADHOUSE; ROUTE 66 STATE PARK.

Britten Truck Stop

(Groom, TX) Long closed, what remains to be seen is a water tower that was placed at the site as an advertising ploy (marked "Britten") during the time the truck stop was in business. The water tower was never properly installed in the ground, causing it to lean markedly, and thereby adding to the visual spectacle.

Britton

A community—now buried within the Oklahoma City limits—that was at one

time on an al-
ternate align-
ment of Route
66 (ALT 66, or
sometimes re-
ferred to as the
"beltline") and distinguished by the presence of the Owl Courts Motel. The Britton
district is reached by turning west onto
Britton Road in northern OKC and then
south on Western or May Avenue (the path
varied over the years). This alignment was
designed to bypass downtown traffic congestion, and it rejoins the primary alignment at 23rd Street, west of the capitol. See
also ALIGNMENT; BYPASS.

Buffalo Ranch
(Afton, OK) A former tourist attraction that
included trained buffalo (bison) and other
animal acts. In the early 2000s the remains
of the ranch were demolished, and a modern truck stop was constructed on the site.
However, even today a few head of buffalo
are kept for nostalgic tourists.

Buffalo Soldiers
A group of several peacetime U.S. Army
regiments organized after the American
Civil War and made up entirely of African-
American troops. They were extremely ac-
tive in the control of hostile Native-Amer-

ican tribes during the "Indian Wars" period from 1866 to the 1890s. Their name is thought to have originated from Native Americans' likening their coarse hair to that of the American bison (or buffalo), large herds of which roamed the Great Plains in that era. There is a museum in Baxter Springs, Kansas, that presents some information about an earlier segregated army regiment that played a role in repulsing Quantrill's Raiders in that area.

Bug Ranch

(Conway, TX) A spoof of the more well-known Cadillac Ranch several miles to the west. Whereas Cadillac Ranch consists of a line of several Cadillac automobiles partially buried in the ground, Bug Ranch substitutes Volkswagen Beetles. Both are open-air displays. See also CADILLAC RANCH.

Bunion Derby

Officially the International Transcontinental Foot Race of 1928. Soon dubbed the Bunion Derby by waggish journalists, the race was organized by promoter C.C. Pyle, and followed the course of U.S. 66 from Southern California to Chicago, and then continued on to New York City, where the race concluded 84 days and more than 3,000 miles after its start. The winner of that race, Andy Payne, grew up on a farm near Foyil, Oklahoma, and there is a bronze statue of him beside a Route 66 alignment near the edge of town. See also ANDY PAYNE.

Bunyon's

(Cicero, IL) Formerly a restaurant special-

izing in hot dogs and featuring a "muffler man" figure out front holding an over-sized hot dog and bun. After the restaurant closed its doors, the muffler man was moved to Atlanta, Illinois, where it remains on display. See also MUFFLER MAN.

Burma Shave

A brand of shaving cream manufactured by the Burma-Vita Company of Minneapolis widely known for its unique highway-side advertising, which was begun in 1927 and continued until 1963. Most advertisements were composed of six signs posted at short intervals. The first five contained a short, often humorous poem or rhyme. The final sign in the series would say simply "Burma Shave." An example is:

Does Your Husband
Misbehave
Grunt and Grumble
Rant and Rave
Shoot the Brute Some
Burma Shave

The first set of Burma Shave signs was erected alongside U.S. 65 near the town of Albert Lea, Minnesota. The campaign came to a close and the signs were taken down in 1963 when the Burma-Vita Company was acquired by Philip Morris, Inc.

Burros

(Oatman, AZ) Small donkeys, particularly those used as pack animals. They are commonly seen roaming the streets of Oatman (actually, there's just the one street—Route 66) where they are fed and otherwise indulged by tourists. Oatman being in mining country, today's burros are descendants of animals used decades ago as beasts of burden and subsequently abandoned.

Business Loop

In many of the larger towns along 66 that have interstate access, the last path of 66 prior to its demise is often marked "Business Loop XX," where XX refers to the number of the interstate in the area. It forms a loop in the sense that it joins the interstate at each end. For example, in Springfield, Missouri, an alignment of Route 66 is posted as Business Loop 44: it leaves westbound I-44 at Glenstone Avenue and heads south, just as 66 did in its day, then it turns right (west) onto Chestnut Expressway and rejoins I-44 on the western outskirts of the city, at Hazeltine. Following such business loops will typically allow the Route 66 explorer to see examples of 66-era motels, gas stations, and the like, but keep in mind that this is only one of (usually) several alignments of 66, and that these loops will always return to the interstate, sometimes abruptly.

Bypass

1. A route (often less direct) that a highway takes in order to avoid areas of higher congestion or other problems. Highways such as Route 66 passed in their earliest days directly along the downtown streets of cities. As populations and automotive traffic grew, "bypass" routes were created that allowed "through" traffic to avoid inner-city congestion. Commonly, the older route would attain the status of "city 66" and the newer bypass alignment would become the primary route. 2. To pass around, or avoid, a

city or other traffic impediment. When the Interstate Highway System was built, it was designed to bypass most cities in order to facilitate steady traffic flow. Many of those towns and cities suffered economically from the subsequent loss of commerce.

Cadillac Ranch

(Amarillo, TX) An outdoor art installation dating from 1974 and comprised of a row of 10 partially buried Cadillac automobiles with their tail fins angling skyward; the artwork is visible from I-40 in a field on the western outskirts of town. It has become the norm that pilgrims to the site bring cans of spray paint and add graffiti

to the cars; periodically the cars are all repainted in a solid color so that this process can begin anew. Popularly considered one of the most distinctive and important features of Route 66, in truth Cadillac Ranch dates from well after U.S. 66 had lost its importance, and so was actually installed in proximity to the Mother Road's successor in the area, Interstate 40. Surprisingly, the whole installation was picked up and moved several years ago in response to encroaching development at its original location, which had been a short distance to the east. The original artwork was commissioned by local tycoon Stanley Marsh 3 and created by a group of collaborators calling themselves the Ant Farm. See also STANLEY MARSH 3; ANT FARM.

Cahokia Mounds
Officially Cahokia Mounds State Historic Site; the location of an ancient Native-American settlement near Collinsville, Illinois, and across the Mississippi River from St. Louis, Missouri. The complex includes the largest man-made mound in North America.

Cajon Pass/Cajon Summit
Cajon Pass is a mountain pass that facilitates crossing the San Gabriel Mountains north of San Bernardino, California, there-

by connecting the Mojave Desert to the north with the Los Angeles Basin to the south. Cajon Summit refers to the highest point of the pass, at over 4,000 feet

(1,200 meters) of elevation, and where the Summit Inn café is located. Although there has been a Summit Inn since the 1930s, the original one sat on an alignment that was bypassed, forcing the move to the current location in the early 1950s.

Campbell's 66 Express

A trucking company that originated in the Route 66 town of Springfield, Missouri, and which is notable for its mascot, Snortin' Norton the camel. See also HUMPIN' TO PLEASE.

Canyon Diablo

1. A seasonal riverbed that was first bridged circa 1915. As a strategic spot, that crossing point formed the nucleus for the Two Guns trading post. See also TWO GUNS. 2. A tiny community in the vicinity of Two Guns.

Caprock
Geological term for a more erosion-resistant rock that overlies a less resistant rock type.

Cars
Disney/Pixar animated feature film released in 2006 and featuring the exploits of an anthropomorphic racing car who accidentally finds himself stranded in the fictional Route 66 town of Radiator Springs. There are a number of buildings, geographical features, and other details in the film that were clearly inspired by actual U.S. 66 locations. See also JOHN LASSETER; ROCK CAFÉ.

Cars Land
(Anaheim, CA) A planned 12-acre expansion of Disney's California Adventure theme park inspired by the Disney/Pixar movie *Cars* and scheduled for completion in 2012. The film, which was released in the summer of 2006, is set partly in a fictional town on Route 66. See also CARS.

Casa Del Desierto
(Barstow, CA) A grand Harvey House hotel, part of which has been converted into the Route 66 Mother

Road Museum; Spanish for "house of the desert." See also HARVEY HOUSE.

Center of the Universe

(Tulsa, OK) In the roadside attraction tradition of "mystery spots," this is a location at the apex of a pedestrian walkway downtown that has odd acoustical properties. Stand on the spot, speak in a normal tone of voice, and your words will strongly reverberate back to you. It's on the Boston Avenue walkway between First and Archer streets.

Central Avenue

(Albuquerque, NM) Central Avenue began carrying Route 66 traffic through Albuquerque beginning in 1937, when the highway was realigned to bypass Santa Fe and pass through Albuquerque east to west. Prior to that time (1926–'36), the highway had entered Albuquerque from the north along Fourth Street. Central Avenue on the east side of town has one of the largest collections of Route 66-era motels anywhere.

Chain

A group of businesses sharing the same name, products, and business plan, which may be owned by an overarching corporation or by any number of franchisees. See also FRANCHISE.

Chain of Rocks Bridge

(St. Louis, MO) Originally a toll bridge constructed in 1929, this bridge later carried Route 66 traffic over the Mississippi River at St. Louis, functioning as a bypass route that avoided downtown congestion. Its Route 66 phase lasted from the late 1930s until 1967, after which it was closed to traffic,  its fate remaining uncertain for decades. In the 1990s it was finally saved from demolition and converted into a pedestrian recreation trail. The bridge is distinctive for its 22-degree bend in the middle, which allows the bridge to offer stronger resistance to the river currents, while also facilitating river navigation.

Cherokee Kid

1. A nickname for Will Rogers, who was part Cherokee Indian. 2. A bronze sculpture of Will Rogers on horseback that stands in his hometown of Oologah, Oklahoma.

Chicago Fire

The Great Fire that consumed most of Chicago in 1871 and which is popularly said to have been caused by Mrs. O'Leary's cow. It is partly to the Great Fire that Chicago owes its rebirth as a center for architecture. The famous Chicago Water Tower is one of the few structures to have survived the blaze and which still stands to this day.

Chicken Boy

(Los Angeles, CA) 1. A former fast-food chicken outlet that did business on Broadway until closing in the early 1980s. 2. An example of a muffler man but with some unique characteristics. This one used to stand on the rooftop of the fast-food place of the same name. It was modified to include the head of a chicken, and the hands, unlike those of most muffler men, come together at the front in order to hold a container (presumably of chicken). Chicken Boy was rescued in 1984 by Amy Inouye (aka Chicken Boy's mom) and has since been re-erected at 5558 N. Figueroa Street (at one time an alignment of Route 66). See also MUFFLER MAN.

Chicken-in-the-Rough

A franchise food business begun in the

1930s by Beverly Osborne and his wife, Rubye. Rather than furnish utensils, diners were encouraged to eat their chicken meals with their fingers, much as they would do at home,

which was innovative for the time. The Osbornes' original restaurant was on Route 66 in Oklahoma City. The idea for the name came from a chance occurrence when the Osbornes were trying to eat a chicken lunch in a moving car; when an abrupt bump caused their meal to scatter, Mrs. Osborne groused that it was "chicken in the rough."

Chief Wolf Robe

See ARROWOOD TRADING POST.

Chisholm Trail

Cattle trail named for Jesse Chisholm, who helped establish and popularize it. It crosses paths with Route 66 in Oklahoma, in the Yukon-to-El Reno vicinity. The trail, which

looms large in the history and lore of America's Old West, ran from southern Texas to Abilene, Kansas, through the corridor now occupied by Interstate 35 and U.S. 81. There are Chisholm Trail museums both to the north and south of 66 in the towns of Kingfisher and Duncan, respectively. Jesse Chisholm's final resting place is north of the Route 66 town of Geary, Oklahoma, at a site called Left Hand Springs Camp.

City of Spires

Nickname for the city of Joliet, Illinois, said to derive from the plethora of churches in the area.

Civilian Conservation Corps (CCC)

An organization initiated during the Depression intended to provide work for young men. Members were put to work performing such duties as road building, park maintenance, and forest management. Many of the structures they built are still extant on Route 66 and elsewhere, and exhibit many of the characteristics typical of Depression-era construction, including Streamline and Deco styling features, and the extensive use of native stone.

Cloverleaf

A highway interchange at which two highways, one crossing over the other, have a series of entrance and exit ramps that, when viewed from above, resemble the outline of a four-leaf clover. Such an interchange enables vehicles to proceed in either direction on either highway without the need to come to a full stop.

Club Café

(Santa Rosa, NM) Now-defunct café that was established in the 1930s and gained notoriety for its billboards featuring a "smiling fat man" logo. See also SMILING FAT MAN.

Coconino Caverns

See GRAND CANYON CAVERNS.

Code Talkers

A group of about 400 individuals from the Navajo tribe employed by the United States armed forces during World War II to convey messages that could not be deciphered by the enemy. The Navajo language is vastly different from other languages of the world, and in the 1940s virtually all speakers of Navajo resided in remote areas of the southwestern United States, preventing the Japanese forces from being able to "crack the code." There is an exhibit in Gallup, New Mexico that tells this very interesting tale. This was such a tightly guarded secret that it was not until 1968 that the operation was declassified, and not until 1982 did the U.S. government publicly honor the efforts of the Navajo code talkers by way of a Presidential Certificate of Recognition. In 2002, a feature film was released, called *Windtalkers*, which tells a fictionalized version of the story.

Thomas Coffin

Artist responsible for creating the tail fin-themed monument outside the Tucumcari (New Mexico) Convention Center.

Coleman Theatre

(Miami, OK) Officially named the Coleman Theatre Beautiful when it was completed in 1929, the Coleman is a combination of Italianate and Spanish Mission architectural styles. In its prime, the Coleman hosted such performers as Sally Rand and Will Rogers. Today, it has been restored (even to the extent of retrieving the original organ) and is once again a performance venue. See also BOLLER BROTHERS (theater designers).

Mary Colter

(1869–1958) One of only a few female American architects in the early twentieth century, Mary Colter completed more than 20 projects for the Fred Harvey Company, for which she was chief architect for several years. Her most renowned creations for Fred Harvey include El Navajo in Gallup, New Mexico (razed in the 1950s), and La Posada in Winslow, Arizona. Colter also created several structures at Grand Canyon National Park. La Posada, in the Route 66 town of Winslow, was beautifully refurbished over the course of several years beginning in the late 1990s. See also HARVEY HOUSE.

Commerce Comet

Early nickname given to baseball star Mickey Mantle; he was raised in the Route 66 town of Commerce, Oklahoma, where his boyhood home still stands.

Concrete

1. A construction material consisting, in its simplest form, of Portland cement, aggregate, and water. See also PORTLAND CEMENT. 2. A frozen confection sold by Ted Drewes Frozen Custard of St. Louis, Missouri. See TED DREWES FROZEN CUSTARD.

Jim Conkle

Mother Road preservation activist who was the master of ceremonies for the 2003 Route 66 Caravan funded by Hampton Inn Hotels. Jim also created the California Route 66 Preservation Foundation, which later evolved into the Route 66 Preserva-

tion Foundation. See also ROUTE 66 PRESERVA-
TION FOUNDATION.

Continental Divide

1. A geologic feature (usually a line of
highly elevated terrain) that causes rain-
fall on one side of it to drain to a different body of water than rain falling on the
other side. In the United States, a line run-
ning through the Rocky Mountains forms
a continental divide (also called the "Great
Divide") separating the Atlantic and Pacific watersheds. 2. A community located
along Route 66 near the point where it
crosses the continental divide (sense #1) in
New Mexico. There was at one time a set
of tourist-oriented service buildings at that
location known collectively as Top o' the
World.

Controlled-Access

See LIMITED-ACCESS.

Cool Springs Camp

A recently refurbished roadside store west
of Kingman, Arizona. For years, the site

was in a state of utter
ruin, consisting of a
pair of stone columns
and little else. The
owner, Ned Leucht-
ner, received the

Cyrus Avery preservation award in 2006 in recognition of his efforts to save it.

Coral Court Motel

This motel was constructed in the early 1940s on Watson Road in greater St. Louis, Missouri, and had several distinguishing features. It was designed in the Streamline-Moderne style—well after that style's peak in the 1930s; construction was of buff-colored ceramic brick with glass-block accents and curved corners; each of the more than 70 units included

an attached garage; the motel was built as a "village" of discrete units rather than as one structure; and, it was named for marine fauna in spite of its Mid-America location. Despite preservationists' efforts to the contrary, the Coral Court was demolished in 1995. However, part of one of the motel's units was retained for display at the Museum of Transportation, not far from where the Coral Court stood for 50-plus years. The site of the motel is now occupied by a housing subdivision named Oak Knoll Manor. See also STREAMLINE MODERNE; MUSEUM OF TRANSPORTATION; OAK KNOLL MANOR. See also the "Need to Know More?" section.

Corn Dog

Generic name for a battered and deep-fried hot dog popularly served on a stick at fairs, carnivals, and similar events. See also COZY DOG DRIVE-IN.

Corridor

A highway, and the area immediately around it, that is influenced by—and is accessible due to—that highway's presence.

Cottage-Style

A type of gas-station design that proliferated in the 1920s and 1930s in response to popular tastes. Prior to the development of the cottage-style station, many fuel vendors were housed in little more than shacks, and they were considered undesirable as neighbors. The larger oil companies— notably Pure Oil Company and architect C.A. Peterson— responded with a design that attempted to blend into a neighborhood by mimicking residential construction. There is a former Phillips 66 station in McLean, Texas, that exemplifies the breed.

Cozy Dog Drive-In

(Springfield, IL) A famous Route 66 eatery in the Illinois capital established by Ed Waldmire, Jr., shortly after World War II that is still run by members of his family to this day. Waldmire is credited by many as being the inventor of the corn dog—a batter-covered hot dog served on a stick, which he dubbed the cozy dog—now a staple at traditional American events such as state and county fairs. In fact, the cozy dog actually premiered at the Illinois State Fair in 1946.

Crusty Cur

The original name Ed Waldmire, Jr., intended for his culinary invention—the battered and deep-fried hot dog—but renamed the cozy dog. See also COZY DOG DRIVE-IN.

Curio

An interesting or unusual object, often art or handicraft. The term derives from the word "curiosity."

Jack Cutberth

(19?–1978) Also known as "Mr. 66," Jack Cutberth was a resident of Clinton, Oklahoma, and extremely active in U.S. 66 associations at both the state and national levels. When the Interstate Highway System began to sound the death knell for Route 66 in the 1950s, Jack Cutberth lobbied in Washington to limit the number of towns that would be completely bypassed by the interstates without access. Those efforts were partially successful, thus saving many communities from near-certain extinction.

Cyrus Avery Award
Named for the Tulsan who did so much to create, number, and determine the routing of Route 66, this award is presented annually to honor a worthy preservation project on the highway. In June of 2007, it was awarded to Old Armory Restorers for their excellent work on the newly refurbished Old Armory Building in Chandler, Oklahoma. That former "basket case" now houses a state-of-the-art interpretive center. See also CYRUS AVERY.

Dairy Queen
A well-established chain of restaurants, originally specializing in soft-serve ice cream, that had its first location in the Route 66 town of Joliet, Illinois, in 1940.

Dead Man's Curve
1. Any winding stretch of road that poses

such a hazard to drivers that it has been the scene of fatal crashes. 2. A sharp curve on Route 66 between the villages of Mesita and Laguna, New Mexico, not far from Owl Rock. See also OWL ROCK.

Angel Delgadillo

The town barber of Seligman, Arizona, for nearly 50 years (a calling that followed in his father's footsteps), Angel was a key force in the formation of the Historic Route 66 Association of Arizona. In 2000, he was honored with the John Steinbeck Award. Today, he operates the Route 66 Visitor Center and Gift Shop, which shares a location with his old barbershop. See also JOHN STEINBECK AWARD.

Juan Delgadillo

(1916-2004) Born in Seligman, Arizona, Juan established the Snow Cap Drive-In in his hometown in the early 1950s after having had a 20-year career with the Santa Fe Railroad. He was well known to travelers for his zany brand of humor, from which no customer to his business was safe. One of his many gags entailed offering patrons ketchup, and then squirting the bottle at them, which would cause the customer to flinch as they were hit with a red string-like substance. Juan and his brother Angel were instrumental in the formation of the

Historic Route 66 Association of Arizona in the 1980s, the first such organization of its kind.

Devil's Elbow

1. A community in central Missouri, east of Waynesville.
2. A bend in the Big Piney River for which the settlement was named; so-called due

to the problems the sharp bend created for river commerce in the area.

Devil's Rope

A nickname for barbed wire, the invention of which was a true milestone in the history of the American West, as it allowed for fencing in spite of the lack of plentiful timber required for more conventional fence construction. There is a museum

dedicated to Devil's Rope in McLean, Texas, which shares a building with a Route 66 exhibit.

Diablo Canyon

See CANYON DIABLO.

Diagonal Highway

A name sometimes used to refer to Route 66; unlike most of the U.S. interstate highways, U.S. 66 does not run strictly east-west or north-south. This fact is a major part of the reason that Route 66 was replaced by not one, but five modern interstates in an effort by highway officials to honor their ideal "grid" system.

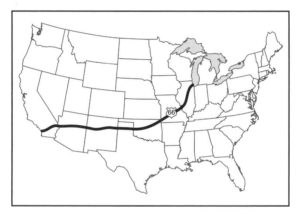

The Diamonds

(Villa Ridge, MO) The present site is actually the restaurant's second location. The original building—once billed as the world's largest restaurant—burned in the

1940s, and the Tri-County Truck Stop now sits on the old site. Later, the Diamonds was re-established at the location you see today. See also TRI-COUNTY TRUCK STOP.

Lester Dill

(1898–1980) Cave entrepreneur whom some say was Missouri's answer to P.T. Barnum. Lester Dill explored caves as a young boy, and by the age of 12 was already conducting tours. He opened Meramec Caverns as a commercial venture in the 1930s after having already held the tour concession at nearby Fisher Cave for a number of years. He is often credited with inventing the bumper sticker, a form of advertising that unsuspecting cave visitors found affixed to their cars after they'd completed their tours. Dill also promoted Meramec Caverns by convincing farmers up and down nearby Route 66 to agree to have their barns painted with the Meramec logo. There are still a few of those advertising barns left for today's tourist to see. See also MERAMEC CAVERNS.

Dinosaur Caverns

Former name for the attraction now called Grand Canyon Caverns, west of Seligman, Arizona. According to some old postcards (circa 1960s), the complex (including caves, motel, campground, airfield, and

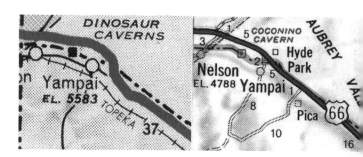

post office) was at one time known as Dinosaur City. On some very old road maps (circa 1940s) the caves appear as Coconino Caverns. See also GRAND CANYON CAVERNS; COCONINO CAVERNS.

Dixie Truckers Home

(McLean, IL) For many years, a tiny hallway in this truck stop served as the Illinois Route 66 Hall of Fame, with several display cases of photos, souvenirs, and other keepsakes. The Hall of Fame was moved to Pontiac, Illinois, upon the opening of the Illinois Route 66 Hall of Fame & Museum in an old firehouse in 2004. The Dixie is still reputed to be the oldest continuously operating truck stop on Route 66.

Dog Iron Ranch

(Oologah, OK) Open to the public, Will Rogers' 400-acre boyhood home includes a house, barn, petting zoo, and more. Oologah is approximately 13 miles from Claremore, site of the Will Rogers Memorial.

Domino

The name of the bovine mascot for Rod's Steak House of Williams, Arizona. Domino is the main design feature both for the restaurant's sign and also for its distinctive die-cut menus.

Jimmy Doolittle

(1896–1993) Record-setting aviator and World War II hero for whom the Mother Road town of Doolittle, Missouri, is named. Although his accomplishments are many, Doolittle is best known for leading the so-called Tokyo Raid in 1942, which, coming only months after the devastating Japanese attack on Pearl Harbor, was a tremendous lift to Allied—particularly American—morale. General Doolittle received numerous honors during his lifetime, and has been enshrined in the Smithsonian Air and Space Museum in Washington, D.C.

Dot's Mini Museum

(Vega, TX) A small collection of buildings near a dead-end segment of Route 66 chock-

full of items collected by "Dot" Leavitt over the years. Dot's family ran Vega Zero Lockers for many years, providing services both for locals and for those traveling on Route 66, including "Jugs Iced Free." Later, Dot carried on the family tradition of kindness to motorists by providing tours of her collection of Mother Road odds and ends. Sadly, Dot passed away in 2006, but some of her children are honoring her memory by carrying on with the mini museum.

Drive-In

1. An outdoor motion-picture theater in which the audience remains seated in their automobiles. 2. A restaurant or café catering to the motoring public that often has carhop and/or walk-up service.

Drive-Thru

A business—most commonly a restaurant or bank—that serves customers in their vehicles by means of a special window. Orders are placed, paid for, and delivered without the customer leaving his or her car. The system was pioneered in the United States in the 1940s, with Red's Giant Hamburg of Springfield, Missouri, claiming to be the first restaurant with a drive-thru window (circa 1947). See also RED'S GIANT HAMBURG.

Dust Bowl

The result of a series of dust storms that stripped much of the central United States of its topsoil in the 1930s, leading to massive migration of farm families out of the affected region, especially Oklahoma. The storms were brought on by a combination of poor farming techniques, the cultivation of marginal lands, and severe drought.

Dynamite Museum

Not a museum per se, but the name given collectively to the group of mock-road-sign "artwork" scattered throughout Amarillo, Texas, and several nearby panhandle towns;

the brainchild of local arts patron Stanley Marsh 3. See also STANLEY MARSH 3.

Ernie Edwards
Founder of the Pig-Hip Restaurant in Broadwell, Illinois. He also served as justice of the peace for many years, a role that provides a legacy of many rich anecdotes. See also PIG-HIP RESTAURANT.

Dwight D. Eisenhower
(1890–1969) The thirty-fourth president of the United States, Eisenhower presided over the establishment of America's Interstate Highway System, which supplanted the older highway system of which U.S. 66 was a part. He had been impressed with the German autobahns he had seen in his army service during World War II, and advocated a similar system here in the U.S. designed to evacuate larger cities in the event of a future war or other national calamity. The resulting legislation took the name National Interstate and Defense Highways Act (1956).

Eisler Brothers
(Riverton, KS) Formally Eisler Brothers' Old Riverton Store; an old-fashioned general store

established in 1925 (prior to the U.S. 66 designation), and run by the same family since 1973. In addition to the staples implied by the term "general store," Eisler Brothers also carries an impressive assortment of Route 66-related merchandise.

El Camino Real

Spanish for "The Royal Road," this term was used to describe any of several roads connecting significant settlements within Spain's colonies. One such road is encountered by Route 66 in New Mexico, where one of the Caminos Real connected Santa Fe with Mexico City. That highway was active in the sixteenth through eighteenth centuries.

El Garces

(Needles, CA) One of the grand Harvey House hotels, constructed in the first decade of the twentieth century. It was retired as a hotel about 1949, but a preservation group was formed (Friends of El Garces) in the 1990s in an attempt to save it from neglect. In 1999, the Friends succeeded in convincing the City of Needles to acquire the property, and renovations are still ongoing. See also HARVEY HOUSE.

El Malpais

Spanish for "badlands." In particular, the

term is used to describe extensive lava fields in western New Mexico through which Route 66 passes. The solidified lava is extremely hard and sharp, making road construction in its vicinity difficult. It is also capable of inflicting severe damage to the footwear of hikers.

El Rancho

Popular Spanish-influenced name given to countless roadside businesses, particularly in the western U.S., during the middle decades of the twentieth century. On today's Route 66, two of the most prominent examples are the El Rancho Hotel/Motel (Gallup, New Mexico) and the El Rancho Motel (Barstow, California). (Spanish: *rancho* = ranch)

El Vado Motel

(Albuquerque, NM) Southwestern adobe-style motel court (circa 1930s) on the western outskirts of the

city, near the Rio Grande. There is an on-going debate within the community as to whether to preserve the motel, or to allow redevelopment of the property.

Eldridge (or Elderidge)

An early name for the town of Alanreed, Texas. The original townsite is north of the current Alanreed. By driving a few miles north on Highway 291, and then west on County Road X, you can find the old Eldridge cemetery.

Rand Elliott

A native of the Route 66 town of Clinton, Oklahoma, and an accomplished architect, Mr. Elliott designed two notable buildings that are must-sees for today's Mother Road traveler: the Oklahoma Route 66 Museum (Clinton, Oklahoma, 1995) and POPS (Arcadia, Oklahoma, 2007). See also POPS.

Escalante Hotel

(Ash Fork, AZ) Former Harvey House hotel that closed in 1948 (later demolished). See also HARVEY HOUSE.

Exotic World

(Helendale, CA) Located on a former goat farm, Exotic World Burlesque Museum & Hall of Fame was a tribute to strippers and exotic dancers, some well-known and some obscure. In 2006, the museum relocated to Las Vegas, Nevada (thoroughly apropos).

Expansion Joint
A device intended to allow for the expansion and contraction of construction materials, sometimes referred to as a control joint. Older concrete sections of Route 66 were equipped with such joints, and their presence is made obvious by the rhythmic thumping they induce from automobile tires.

Fat Man
See SMILING FAT MAN.

First Motel in Texas
See LAST MOTEL IN TEXAS.

Flagstone Capital of the World
Nickname for the town of Ash Fork, Arizona, also known by the more modest "Flagstone Capital of the United States." Flagstone is a sedimentary rock that can be cleaved into flat stones useful for paving.

Folk Art
Art- or craftwork that is created by someone without formal artistic training; also known as "naïve" or "outsider" art (especially within the fine art community). Folk art is usually completed primarily for the

satisfaction of the artist, and not intended for any commercial market. Ed Galloway's Totem Pole Park is a prime example. See NATHAN "ED" GALLOWAY; TOTEM POLE PARK.

Fort Leonard Wood

U.S. Army post (named for a former chief of staff) established in 1940 near the Route 66 town of Waynesville, Missouri. The post was a significant basic-training center during World War II, and the resulting high traffic on nearby 66 led to the widening of the highway through the area, including the well-known "Hooker Cut," an early example of road construction techniques that became so common in the later "interstate" era. See also HOOKER CUT.

Fort Reno

A former army installation west of El Reno, Oklahoma, known for its rearing of horses for the United States Army during the pre-mechanized era. Today, some of the ruins of Fort Reno are open for touring by the public, and there is a cemetery that holds the remains of several World War II prisoners of war.

Franchise

Franchise businesses are ones in which the operator pays fees to a larger company for the rights to sell an established (and standardized) product using standardized materials and methods. Often, the franchise holder turns the day-to-day operations of the business over to hired help. Synonym: chain. Contrast this with mom-and-pop. See also CHAIN; MOM-AND-POP.

Frankoma Pottery

(Sapulpa, OK) Pottery company with a distinctive style that has been operating on an old alignment of Route 66 since the 1930s.

Fray Marcos Hotel

(Williams, AZ) A former Harvey House hotel that sees duty today as the depot for the Grand Canyon Railway. The railway offers excursions to Grand Canyon National Park from here. See also HARVEY HOUSE.

"Friends Don't Let Friends Drive the Interstate"

Proprietary pro-Route 66 slogan originated by Drew and Lauren Knowles of Fort Worth, Texas, and used in a popular T-shirt design. The slogan also appears (translated into Esperanto) on the official crest for Route66 University.com, where it reads "Amikos ne lasi amikos veturilo ju autovojo." The same philosophy is espoused in one of Michael Wallis' favorite expressions: "Life begins at the off-ramp."

Frog Rock
(Waynesville, MO) A rocky outcropping on the side of a hill that vaguely resembles a frog in shape, Frog Rock is periodically re-painted in appropriate colors to enhance the illusion.

Frozen Custard
A frozen dessert similar to ice cream, but containing eggs in addition to the cream and sugar found in ice cream. Additionally, the product is relatively dense, with less air mixed in when compared to ice cream. See also TED DREWES FROZEN CUSTARD; CONCRETE.

Galena
A grayish mineral ore, composed chiefly of lead sulfate (PbS), from which metallic lead is extracted. The Route 66 town of Galena, Kansas, owes its name to this local resource.

Nathan "Ed" Galloway
(1880–1962) Creator of the folk-art collection now known as Totem Pole Park just

off Route 66 in Foyil, Oklahoma. Shortly after moving to Foyil in the 1930s, Ed began building and sculpting several Native-American-inspired structures, including an eleven-sided "Fiddle House" in which to store the hundreds of fiddles he carved, as well as a 90-foot-tall hollow totem pole completed in 1948. Galloway's heirs donated the property in 1989 to the Rogers County Historical Society, which now maintains the park. See also TOTEM POLE PARK.

Gascozark

1. A community in western Pulaski County, Missouri, that includes the Gascozark Trading Post. 2. A region of central Missouri that derives its name from the Gasconade River and the Ozark Plateau.

Gay Parita

1. A gasoline station that opened circa 1930 at what is now Paris Springs, Missouri. The station was established by Fred Mason and named in part for his wife, Gay Mason. (The origin of the "parita" portion of the name is obscure, but it is interesting to note that there was once

a dance hall named the Gay Parita in the town of Carona, in southeastern Kansas.) 2. A small community named for the station (see #1) at its center. 3. A reproduction gasoline station built on the same site and hosted by Gary Turner as a tribute to Route 66's past. The property includes the original garage constructed of native stone.

Gemini Giant

(Wilmington, IL) A former "muffler man" later transformed into a space traveler, this figure stands outside the Launching Pad Drive-In on Highway 66. These giant figures were once common all over preinterstate American roadsides. See also MUFFLER MAN.

Geodesic Dome

A near-spherical structure composed of struts and popularized by R. Buckminster Fuller in the 1940s. It is the only man-made structure that becomes stronger as it is increased in size. There are some trading

posts on Route 66 in Arizona incorporating geodesic domes in their designs, an example being the Meteor City Trading Post.

"Get Your Kicks on Route 66"

Well-known Mother Road slogan based upon the refrain from composer Bobby Troup's hit song "Route 66," which he wrote in 1946 during a cross-country trip on the highway. See also BOBBY TROUP.

Ghost Light (or Spooklight)

In northeastern Oklahoma, near the Missouri border, there have been reports for many years of mysterious lights. You can obtain directions to the rather isolated area by asking locally, but be forewarned that area police discourage such trips.

Ghost Town

1. A town that has been completely deserted and is no longer inhabited by its hu-

man population.
2. A town that,
after reaching a
population peak,
has entered a pe-
riod of decline,
such that its resi-
dents and local
businesses num-
ber only a fraction of what they did in the
past. In this sense, there are a large number of ghost towns to be experienced on
Route 66.

Glorieta Pass
Location in New Mexico for which a handful of American Civil War battles of 1862
were named, collectively known as the
Battle of Glorieta Pass. Those events oc-
curred at a series of sites along the Santa Fe
Trail, which Route 66 follows very closely
in the vicinity.

Golden Driller
(Tulsa, OK) A 76-foot-tall statue of an
oil worker that stands at the Tulsa fairgrounds.

Golden Spread
An informal geographic region roughly
centered on the Texas Panhandle. The
term is thought to have been coined by

an Amarillo radio announcer in the 1950s as an expression of pride in the area's abundant resources. The term has been incorporated into the names of numerous businesses, chambers of commerce, and other organizations in the region that continue to use it to this day. Until the 1990s, there was a pair of matching motels on the east and west outskirts of Groom, Texas bearing the name Golden Spread Motel.

Gouge-Eye

A former name for the community of Alanreed, Texas, said to have originated with an ugly brawl.

Grade

The height (or elevation) of the ground at a given location, often expressed as distance above sea level. In road building, when two intersecting roads meet "at grade," it means that they are on the same level, usually the surface of the ground. Various types of overpasses have been developed so that roads (including railroads) intersect at different grades in order to facilitate traffic flow.

Shellee Graham

An accomplished photographer with a popular traveling exhibition called Return to Route 66: Photographs from the Mother Road, Shellee is best known for her devoted study of the Coral Court Motel in St. Louis, resulting in her book *Tales from the Coral Court: Photos and Stories From a Lost Route 66 Landmark*, now the definitive source for information on this unique motel. In 2005, she was the recipient of the prestigious John Steinbeck Award. See also JOHN STEINBECK AWARD.

Grand Canyon Caverns

A tourist attraction east of Peach Springs, Arizona. The caverns were previously known as Dinosaur Caverns, and before that, Coconino Caverns. See also DINOSAUR CAVERNS; COCONINO CAVERNS.

The Grapes of Wrath

A novel by John Steinbeck (and later a film) describing the Depression-era flight of "Okies" along Route 66 to escape Dust Bowl conditions. It was in this book that Steinbeck coined the name Mother Road to refer to U.S. 66. Several scenes in the film were actually shot on location along the highway.

Green Grow the Lilacs

1. An Irish folk song popular in the nineteenth century. 2. A play by Lynn Riggs that formed the basis for the 1940s musical entitled *Oklahoma!* Lynn Riggs was from the Route 66 town of Claremore, Oklahoma, and there is a small museum there dedicated to his memory.

Lucille Hamons

(1915–2000) Proprietress of a gas station and tourist court business at Provine, a highway junction just south of Hydro, Oklahoma, on U.S. 66. Lucille (as she was known to modern-day Mother Roaders) ran what eventually came to be known simply as "Lucille's" for nearly 60 years, beginning in 1941. She was a welcoming friend to all travelers, earning her the nickname that would be used in the title of her memoirs. That book, published in 1997, was called *Lucille, Mother of the Mother Road.*

Fred Harvey

(1835–1901) The entrepreneur who, through a business agreement with the Santa Fe Railroad, established a series of hotels and restaurants closely associated with the railroad's depots throughout the American Southwest. See also HARVEY HOUSE.

Harvey Girl

A young woman recruited by the Fred Harvey Company to work in one of the company's railroad-connected restaurants. To qualify, the woman needed to be "of good moral character," and was required to sign a contract stipulating that she not marry and that she strictly adhere to all of the Harvey Company rules during her term of employment. In 1946, Metro-Goldwyn-Mayer released a motion picture starring Judy Garland, entitled *Harvey Girls*.

Harvey House

A chain of luxurious hotels and dining facilities started by the Fred Harvey Company, which contracted with the Santa Fe Railroad to provide these services for railroad patrons. They are of interest for Mother Road travelers due to the fact that they are emblematic of a lifestyle that was essentially usurped by the growth of automobile travel, much as Route 66 and her ilk were later supplanted by the Interstate Highway System and affordable air travel; the company is intimately involved with the Atchison, Topeka & Santa Fe, the railroad whose main trunk Route 66 parallels through much of the American Southwest, particularly New Mexico, Arizona, and California; and, many of the remaining Harvey Houses are outstanding architectural jewels in their own right. The grand Harvey House hotels of the Southwest were given names as exotic as their locales: La Fonda in Santa Fe, Alvarado in Albuquerque, and El Navajo in Gallup, New Mexico; La Posada in Winslow, Fray Marcos in Williams, and Havasu in Seligman, Arizona; El Tovar at the Grand Canyon; and El Garces in Needles, California.

Havasu

(Seligman, AZ) The name of the Harvey House hotel established at Seligman, Arizona, circa 1890. The name is taken from the local Havasupai Native-American tribe. In 2005, an organization called Friends of the Havasu was established in order to save and restore the property.

Havasupai

Native-American tribe living in the Grand Canyon area of Arizona. The tribe operates the Havasupai Lodge on their reservation along the canyon's south rim, accessible from Route 66 near Peach Springs.

Hells Angels

World-famous motorcycle club that was first organized in Fontana, California, in March of 1948. The name (which officially no longer contains an apostrophe) was borrowed from an American air squadron of World War II, and was also the title of a motion picture released in 1927 starring Jean Harlow.

Henry's Rabbit Ranch

(Staunton, IL) A latter-day Route 66 visitor center that includes a collection of vintage "Humpin' to Please" truck trailers from the Campbell's 66 Express trucking company. See also HUMPIN' TO PLEASE.

"Here It Is!"

1. (Joseph City, AZ) Simple phrase emblazoned on a billboard across the highway from the Jack Rabbit Trading Post; the billboard is one of the most iconic sights along Route 66. In its heyday, the Jack Rabbit Trading Post had many smaller signs posted for many miles in both directions in order to build anticipation for the motorist's eventual arrival here. See also JACK RABBIT TRADING POST. 2. A popular—and useful—series of eight maps designed to help today's explorer successfully follow Route 66.

"Here We Are on Route 66"

Caption found on a popular postcard from the Route 66 era; that card and caption gained new currency with the publication of Michael Wallis' *Route 66: The Mother Road*, where the postcard is used in the book's cover design.

Hinton Junction

A highway inter-change just east of Bridgeport, Oklahoma, that signals a turnoff for the town of Hinton to the south via U.S. 281. There is a ru-inous café at the site that locals say  once functioned as a bus station.

Hofmann Tower

(Lyons, IL) An eight-story tower beside the Des Plaines River currently housing a museum operated by the Lyons Historical Commission. The building was construct-ed circa 1908. There is also an adjacent Riverwalk.

Hooker Cut

A large gash cut into the earth near the town of Hooker, Missouri, when U.S. 66 was upgraded to a four-lane di-vided highway through this area during the ear-ly 1940s. At the time, the Hooker Cut was consid-

ered unique and different as far as road-building techniques go; however, such cuts have become commonplace today in the "interstate highway" era.

Hopi

Native-American tribe whose reservation, in northeastern Arizona, is completely surrounded by the Navajo reservation, which extends into three states. The Hopi Nation is in the Painted Desert area, north of the Route 66 town of Winslow, Arizona. The Hopi are noted for their kachina dolls, which were at one time a staple of roadside trading posts in this part of the country.

Horseradish Capital

Collinsville, Illinois is best-known to roadies as the home of the World's Largest Catsup Bottle. However, the locals who feel such claims to fame are undignified came up with the Horseradish Capital nickname to divert attention to a more serious asset of the area. Southern Illinois, of which Collinsville is a part, produces about 80 percent of the world's horseradish crop. Each June, Collinsville hosts the International Horseradish Festival in celebration of this distinction. See also WORLD'S LARGEST CATSUP BOTTLE.

Hualapai

Native-American tribe whose headquarters are in the Route 66 town of Peach Springs, Arizona. The Hualapai made lots of headlines when their Grand Canyon Skywalk, a glass-bottomed observation platform mounted on the side of their portion of the Grand Canyon, was completed in March of 2007.

Edwin Hubble

(1889–1953) Astronomer for whom the Hubble Space Telescope was named. There is a scale model of the telescope on the courthouse lawn in the Route 66 town of Marshfield, Missouri, his birthplace.

Hula Ville (or Hulaville)

(Hesperia, CA) An informal roadside destination founded by Miles Mahan, a retired carnival worker, beginning in the 1950s. Hula Ville got its name from one of the largest artifacts on display there, a sign depicting a hula dancer, which Mr. Ma-

han had found in a refuse pile. Hula Ville also included numerous homemade signs and an equal number of "cactuses" Mahan constructed from discarded bottles. When Mr. Mahan fell into ill health in the 1990s, the California Route 66 Museum in Victorville obtained many of the displays and placed them in its collection. The museum also has a scale-model reproduction of Hula Ville so that today's visitor can get a better taste of what the whole property looked like.

Humdinger

(Seligman, AZ) There is a small, hand-painted sign on an exterior wall of the Snow Cap Drive-In advertising this frozen drink.

Humpin' to Please

Slogan used by the Campbell's 66 Express trucking company in connection with their mascot, Snortin' Norton. See also SNORTIN' NORTON.

Indian Day School

The name of a short film, one of the first produced using Thomas Edison's Kinetoscope, an early motion-picture camera. The film was made at Isleta Pueblo, a village on Route 66 in New Mexico.

Indian Territory

Prior to Oklahoma's attainment of statehood in the early twentieth century, it was known officially as Indian Territory. Thus, many older documents and ephemera still existing today include town references such as "Guthrie, I.T."

Interstate
The use of the term "interstate" can be confusing, or at least ambiguous. Today, most people say "interstate" to refer to our modern system of limited-access freeways—with their red-and-blue markers and large green exit signs—and this usage is entirely correct. The problem arises from the fact that the older system of highways, of which U.S. 66 was a part, were also officially called "interstate highways," as they crossed state lines and were regulated at the federal level.

Jack Rabbit Trading Post
(Joseph City, AZ) The subject of the most famous advertising billboard on Route 66. There is a jackrabbit statuette on the property which is a long-popular photographic prop. See also "HERE IT IS!"

Jericho Gap
In the early years of Route 66's existence (1920s-'30s), not all portions of the highway were paved. One such "gap" between paved portions of U.S. 66 was in Texas, near the small community of Jericho. This fact was particularly problematic for early motorists, since the local soil—suitably referred to as black gumbo—becomes nearly impassable when drenched with rain. Anecdotal accounts suggest that area

residents may have deliberately doused the roads with water at night in order to make a few extra dollars pulling stranded motorists out of the quagmire with tractors or mule teams. Eventually the Jericho Gap stretch of highway was improved and re-routed a little to the north. What remains of the community of Jericho lies just south of present-day Interstate 40 near the junction of Texas State Highway 70.

Jimtown
Former name for the town of Miami, Oklahoma, stemming from the fact that at the time there were four Jims living in the area.

Joad
The name of the family making their way west from Oklahoma to California on Route 66 in John Steinbeck's novel *The Grapes of Wrath*. See THE GRAPES OF WRATH.

John Steinbeck Award

From 1996 to 2005, this award was presented by the National Historic Route 66 Federation and the author's heirs to individuals who had made a significant contribution to the continuation of Route 66 as a cultural resource. Recipients of the award are Michael Wallis, presented at Landergin, Texas, 1996; Tom Teague, Amarillo, Texas, 1998; Angel Delgadillo, Kingman, Arizona, 2000; Jim Ross, Albuquerque, New Mexico, 2001; John and Lenore Weiss, Springfield, Illinois, 2002; Jeff Meyer, Springfield, Illinois, 2003; Bob Waldmire, Tulsa, Oklahoma, 2004; and Shellee Graham, San Bernardino, California, 2005.

John's Modern Cabins

A grouping of long-disused tourist cabins on a bypassed segment of Route 66 east of Arlington, Missouri. Despite the name "modern," the cabins are examples of some of the more spartan accommodations to be had, having been served by an outhouse. The remaining struc-

tures are severely damaged and are slowly returning to the earth.

Scott Joplin
(1868–1917) Self-taught American ragtime composer and pianist. He lived in Saint Louis, Missouri, for several years, and his residence is now open to the public (Scott Joplin House State Historic Site).

Kicks
Fun; thrills. The word is forever associated with Route 66 due to Bobby Troup's using it—for its rhyming quality, of course—in his signature song, "(Get Your Kicks on) Route 66."

KiMo Theatre
(Albuquerque, NM) A theater in downtown Albuquerque dating from 1927 designed by the Boller Brothers architectural firm in a style dubbed Pueblo Deco, and featuring finely detailed murals and terra-cotta buffalo skull wall sconces. Some say the KiMo is haunted by the spirit of a young boy who died there in an accident in the 1950s. See also BOLLER BROTHERS.

David and Mary Lou Knudson
Cofounders of the National Historic Route 66 Federation in 1994, the Knudsons were instrumental in the Mother Road's notice-

able gathering of momentum in the 1990s. Through their organization, they brought unity and common purpose to what had been scattered preservation efforts without central vision. It was largely as a result of their tireless efforts that a congressional bill was introduced and passed, which in 1999 resulted in the Route 66 Corridor Preservation Program. In 2006, they were awarded the Founder's Award at an event in Clinton, Oklahoma.

Kozlowski's Ranch

A stagecoach stop on the Santa Fe Trail, near Pecos, New Mexico, that played a small role in a handful of battles of the American Civil War. It was made a part of Pecos National Historical Park in 1990, but as yet has not been opened to the public. See also GLORIETA PASS.

La Bajada Hill

A steep grade on an early alignment of Route 66 between Santa Fe and Albuquerque, New Mexico, which necessitated that that part of the highway be constructed with numerous switchbacks. Today, the old road over La Bajada Hill is not driveable. See also SWITCHBACK.

La Cita

(Tucumcari, NM) A restaurant exhibiting

mimetic (or programmatic) architecture, La Cita's front entrance was designed in the shape of a traditional Mexican sombrero. Like many businesses on old Route 66, La Cita has fallen on hard times and sporadically closes down and reopens for periods. See also MIMETIC.

La Fonda

(Santa Fe, NM) A hotel located on the central plaza of New Mexico's capital city, La Fonda (circa 1920) is built on the site of a much older inn that once acted as the de facto end of the Santa Fe Trail.

La Posada

(Winslow, AZ) One of several Harvey House hotels strung along the Atchison, Topeka & Santa Fe Railroad (which paralleled Route 66), La Posada is considered to be one of the finest works of architect Mary Colter. See also HARVEY HOUSE; MARY COLTER.

Lake Michigan

Third-largest of the Great Lakes, and the city of Chicago's reason for being. U.S. 66's eastern terminus is the proverbial "stone's throw" from the shore of Lake Michigan (Jackson Boulevard at Lake Shore Drive).

Lake Overholser

A man-made body of water just west of Oklahoma City, Oklahoma, and named for one of the city's mayors, Ed Overholser.

John Lasseter

Producer of the Disney/Pixar feature film *Cars* and recipient of the Will Rogers Award in 2006.

Last Motel in Texas

(Glenrio, TX) A motel just east of the Texas-New Mexico state line whose sign informed westbound travelers that it was the last such service before leaving the state. The opposite side of the sign, facing eastbound travelers, said "First Motel in Texas."

Launching Pad Drive-In

(Wilmington, IL) A roadside café operat-

ing since the 1960s notable for its popular symbol, the Gemini Giant. See also GEMINI GIANT; MUFFLER MAN.

Leaning Water Tower
See BRITTEN TRUCK STOP.

Bob and Ramona Lehman
Proprietors of the Munger Moss Motel for more than 35 years (1971–present). The Lehmans are well-regarded as avid supporters of Mother Road events and travelers, and they received the Route 66 Business of the Year Award in 2006.

Liar's Table
1. A table, often extra large and strategically placed, at which restaurant patrons can meet and "shoot the bull." 2. Such a gathering as described in sense #1.

Limited-Access (or Controlled-Access)
Descriptive of a type of road to which access from other roads and/or adjacent properties is limited; i.e., access to the road in question is only available at select interchanges or ramps built for that purpose. In the United States, such roads go by a variety of names, including freeway, expressway, interstate, parkway, and turnpike; also, the use of these names may vary from one jurisdiction to another. It was the limited-access character of the modern Interstate Highway System that sounded the death knell for so many businesses that relied on Route 66 traffic for their livelihoods, since

they were not positioned near the newly created (and relatively few) access points.

Abraham Lincoln

The sixteenth president of the United States, Mr. Lincoln resided and practiced law in the Route 66 town of Springfield, Illinois, where there are numerous sites significant to his life. His family mausoleum is located in Springfield's Oak Ridge Cemetery.

Lincoln Highway

One of the many "named" highways in the years before they were organized by number, the Lin-

coln Highway was America's first coast-to-coast highway, having its genesis in the second decade of the twentieth century. Indicative of the highway's position in American culture is the fact that a brand of cigars elected to co-opt the name (see illustration). Like Route 66, the Lincoln has benefited from a resurgence in interest in historic roadways, as evidenced by the establishment of the Lincoln Highway Association in the 1990s. See also the "Need to Know More?" section.

Llano Estacado

Literally "staked plain." An area mostly

devoid of natural landmarks that received its name from the fact that Spanish explorers drove stakes into the ground as navigational aids. An alternative origin for the name states that it was named for the palisade-like appearance of some cliffs near the Canadian River. Route 66 passes through the Llano Estacado beginning in the Texas Panhandle and continuing until east of the Rio Grande valley. [Spanish: *llano* = plain + *estacado* = staked]

Longhorn Ranch
An Old-West-style town built as a tourist attraction not far from Clines Corners, New Mexico. It also included travelers' services, such as a motel, gas station, café, etc.

Looff Hippodrome
(Santa Monica, CA) A historic building on the Santa Monica Pier that, since its construction in 1915, has housed a succession of hand-carved carousels, the latest of which was made in 1922. [Latin: *Hippo* = horse]

Lou Mitchell's Restaurant
(Chicago, IL) A restaurant in downtown Chicago (Jackson Street) on an eastbound-only section of Route 66. Formerly known as Mitchell's Cupboard, it has been in its present location since the early 1940s.

Lucille's

(Hydro, OK) Common name for the small store operated by Lucille Hamons, aka Mother of the Mother Road. See also LUCILLE HAMONS; PROVINE.

Macadam

A type of road construction named for its originator, John L. MacAdam, in the nineteenth century. It consists of a crowned subsurface (for drainage) covered with multiple layers of irregularly shaped aggregate pressed into place. Later, as automotive travel became more commonplace, higher speeds created the problem of dust clouds. This problem was effectively solved by adding tar to the surface to seal it, resulting in tarmac.

Madonna of the Trail

Any of several stone monuments placed along the National Old Trails Highway between Washington, D.C., and Los Angeles, California. In the early 1920s, the National Society of the Daughters of the American Revolution (DAR) commissioned the design, casting, and placement of 12 monuments commemorating the spirit of the pioneer woman, with one to be placed in each

of the 12 states through which the designated trail passed. Two of those monuments were placed on what would later become U.S. 66, in Albuquerque, New Mexico, and Upland, California. From east to west, the other 10 monuments were dedicated in Bethesda, Maryland; Beallsville, Pennsylvania; Wheeling, West Virginia; Springfield, Ohio; Richmond, Indiana; Vandalia, Illinois; Lexington, Missouri; Council Grove, Kansas; Lamar, Colorado; and Springerville, Arizona.

Miles Mahan

Builder of Hula Ville. Mr. Mahan had no relatives, so when he fell ill as a nonagenarian and could no longer maintain his property, the California Route 66 Museum (Victorville) intervened and absorbed many of Mr. Mahan's creations into its collection in order to preserve the memory for today's roadies. See also HULA VILLE.

Main Street of America

A nickname given to U.S. 66 and used for many years in promotional materials developed to encourage travel on the highway. In the earlier years of its existence, Route 66 (and other highways like her) passed through most cities along their downtown streets, making the nickname quite apt.

Marie Foundations

(McLean, TX) Undergarment company that used to operate in the building now occupied by twin museums celebrating Devil's Rope (barbed wire) and Route 66. See also DEVIL'S ROPE.

Stanley Marsh 3

A wealthy eccentric of Amarillo, Texas, Mr. Marsh is best known for having been the financial collaborator for the outdoor art installation known as Cadillac Ranch, consisting of 10 Cadillac automobiles partially buried in the ground beside Interstate 40 on the western outskirts of Amarillo. Note that the "3" is his preferred designation, and not the more traditional "III." Marsh is also the backer for the Dynamite Museum. See also CADILLAC RANCH; DYNAMITE MUSEUM.

Elmer McCurdy

(1880–1911) A small-time Oklahoma outlaw who gained fame posthumously for

his corpse having seen duty as a carnival prop. According to the story, he was killed in 1911 and, due to odd circumstances, was mummified rather than simply embalmed and interred. His mummy changed hands several times over the years, and was finally discovered in the 1970s in a Los Angeles-area funhouse. He was finally laid to rest in a Guthrie, Oklahoma cemetery in 1977. See also the "Need to Know More?" section

McLain Rogers Park

(Clinton, OK) A city park beside an early alignment of Route 66. The park is noted both

for its neon-illuminated arched entryway and for its Depression-era outdoor amphitheater.

Meadow Gold

A brand name, part of Beatrice Foods. Notable because there was an enormous "Meadow Gold" neon sign in Tulsa, Okla-

homa, at the southwest corner of 11th Avenue (Route 66) and Lewis. When the owner of the building on which the sign was mounted announced his intention to remove the icon, there was a ground-swell of local support for the sign's preservation in 2004. Those preservation efforts led to the sign's dismantling and storage, and the identification of a new site for its eventual reassembly and display.

Mediocre Music Makers

A two-person performance group comprised of Harley and Annabelle Russell of Erick, Oklahoma. They entertain Mother Road travelers in their Sandhills Curiosity Shop with music, singing, and endless humor, and all for no particular fee (though tips are welcome).

Meramec Caverns

(Stanton, MO) First opened commercially

in the 1930s, Meramec Caverns is a tourist attraction just a few miles southeast of Stanton, Missouri (via State Highway W), billing itself as "The Greatest Show Under the Earth." The caverns are well known due in part to the fact that many barns along U.S. 66 were painted as advertising billboards for the caves, a few examples of which still remain. In addition to the caves themselves, Meramec Caverns offers tourists a campground, motel, boating, and gold panning. See also LESTER DILL.

Mesa

Spanish for "table," a mesa is a landscape feature consisting of a raised area of land with a flat top and steep, cliff-like sides. Mesas are common features in the southwestern United States.

Meteor City

1. An I-40 exit west of Winslow, Arizona, and near the Meteor Crater. See also METEOR CRATER. 2. A small trading post at the same exit that is comprised partly of a geodesic dome.

Meteor Crater

1. (lower case) Any bowl-shaped depression caused by the impact of a meteor. 2. (upper case) A large crater, nearly one mile in diameter, located just off Route 66 west of Winslow, Arizona, and determined to have been caused by a meteor's impact approximately 50,000 years ago. The crater is privately owned and operated and is accessible to visitors.

Jeff Meyer

Recipient of the John Steinbeck Award in 2003. Jeff has been traveling Route 66 frequently for many years, meeting and greeting the various businesspeople and fellow adventurers all along the highway—so much so that he has been dubbed the "Ambassador of the Mother Road."

Miami

City in northeastern Oklahoma that is home to the Coleman Theatre; named for the American Indian tribe of the same name and pronounced my-AM-uh. Miami is also known for the two distinct stretches of half-width highway pavement found nearby. See also SIDEWALK HIGHWAY; COLEMAN THEATRE.

Midpoint Café

(Adrian, TX) A restaurant near the geographical midpoint of U.S. 66 that is known for serving "ugly crust pies." There is a small monument directly across the street providing a "midpoint of the route" photo opportunity. See also UGLY CRUST PIES.

Milk Bottle Building

(Oklahoma City, OK) A small wedge-shaped building on an older highway alignment (Classen Avenue) that has an over-sized replica of a

milk bottle on the roof. The building has housed many types of businesses over the years, and the eye-catching milk bottle has been painted with different logos over its lifespan.

The Mill

(Lincoln, IL) Originally named the Blue Mill, this restaurant was first established in the 1920s. The exterior of the building was made to resemble a Dutch-style wind-mill, including a set of lighted blades that actually turned. Part of the build-ing consists of an army barracks that was salvaged from Camp Ellis when it was deactivated in the aftermath of World War II. Today, the exte-

rior includes a sign that states "Home of the Schnitzel Since 1945." After sitting dormant for many years, an effort was initiated in 2007 to save The Mill from the wrecking ball and restore it as a museum.

Roger Miller

(1936–1992) An American singer, songwriter, and musician, Miller grew up in the small Mother Road town of Erick, Oklahoma, where today one can find both a Roger Miller Boulevard and Roger Miller Museum. His most famous song, for which he won a Grammy Award in 1965, is "King of the Road."

Mimetic

Used in describing a type of architecture, once common on the American roadside, wherein the form of the building was physically suggestive of the type of business conducted there; also called programmatic architecture. More broadly, the term can be used to refer to virtually any building that defies common conventions and seeks to mimic something other than a building. One of the most famous examples was Los Angeles's Brown Derby restaurant.

Mom-and-Pop

Any business owned and operated by a family, often a married couple, rather than by a larger business entity; especially where the owners are on the premises each day and personally see to the details of daily operations.

Mormon Trail
In the mid-1800s, the Mormon community established a migratory trail between

their headquarters in Salt Lake City, Utah, and the Los Angeles area of California (they had hopes of converting the Native-American tribes inhabiting the area). Although the Mormons eventually gave up the project and retreated to Utah, there are some commemorative markers very near Route 66 in the Cajon Summit area.

Motel
A form of travelers' lodging in which each room is accessed directly from the parking area for maximum convenience of those traveling by automobile; its derivation is assumed to be a shortening of MOtor hoTEL. Although "motel" is the commonly accepted term today, the preferred term has evolved through a number of stages

over the years: tourist cottages, tourist court, motor village, auto court, and motor lodge, to name only a few.

Mother Jones

(1 8 3 7 – 1 9 3 0) Thought to be the inspiration for the folk song "She'll Be Coming 'Round the Mountain," Mary Harris "Mother" Jones was a well-known labor organizer in the early years of the twentieth century, and remained active in that role well into old age. She earned the nickname "most dangerous woman in America" during a confrontation with the district attorney of West Virginia. Her gravesite is in the town cemetery of the Route 66 community of Mount Olive, Illinois.

Mother Road

One of many nicknames given to Route 66; first coinage attributed to John Steinbeck, author of the dark Depression-era tale *The Grapes of Wrath*, wherein Oklahomans fleeing the Dust Bowl utilize Route 66 (the Mother Road) in making their way westward. See also *THE GRAPES OF WRATH*.

Muffler Man

Beginning roughly in 1960, American road-sides began to be dotted with 20-foot-tall advertising gimmicks now commonly referred to as "muffler men." Each figure typically had one upturned and one downturned hand, originally designed to hold a tool such as a hammer or axe. Most commonly, they were seen outside automotive-related businesses, and quite often held an oversized muffler—thus the nickname. No one knows just how many of these giants might once have stood beside U.S. 66, but today there are two notable examples in Wilmington and Atlanta, Illinois. See also BUNYON'S; GEMINI GIANT.

Mule Trading Post

(Rolla, MO) This trading post on the east side of town features an animated neon sign. The sign depicts the head and neck of a mule, and the animation feature causes the ears to flap. In 2007, the owners restored and erected one of two "hillbilly" signs on the property. The hillbilly comes from an earlier business that originated in Devil's Elbow.

Munger Moss Motel

(Lebanon, MO) The Munger Moss Sandwich Shop opened in Devil's Elbow, Missouri circa 1940. The curious name comes

from the joining of two different surnames—Munger and Moss. When that loop of highway was bypassed during WWII, the owners bought property in Lebanon on which to operate their business, eventually—in 1946—adding motel rooms. The motel was obtained by the Lehmans in 1971 and has been run by them ever since. There is a great collection of antique toy trucks on display in the motel's lobby area. See also BOB AND RAMONA LEHMAN.

Museum Club

(Flagstaff, AZ) A circa-1931 roadhouse that

started out housing a taxidermy collection and known for a time as the Dean Eldridge Museum.

Museum of Transportation
(Kirkwood, MO) This museum in suburban St. Louis has many, many exhibits of interest to roadies, but the most important one for Route 66 pilgrims is the partial motel room from the Coral Court, a large 1940s-era motel complex that was demolished to make room for a housing subdivision. See also CORAL COURT; OAK KNOLL MANOR.

Museums
With the resurgence of interest in Route 66 that has taken place since the early 1990s, several museums have sprung up along the highway that today's Route 66 explorer may find informative and entertaining. They run the gamut from simple assemblages based upon one person's personal collection of memorabilia, to others with state support and elaborate facilities that use modern technology to "tell the story of the Mother Road." Each has its own endearing qualities, and deserves and appreciates your patronage.

National Historic Route 66 Federation
Established in 1994 by David and Mary Lou Knudson, the Federation is a nonprofit

organization that seeks to obtain the governmental and private support needed to preserve significant features and revitalize communities along Route 66 in all eight states through which the highway passed. The Federation also publishes a newsletter, the *Federation News*, four times per year. See also DAVID AND MARY LOU KNUDSON.

National Register
Short for the National Register of Historic Places, America's official list of properties, sites, and other resources deemed worthy of preservation. The program is administered by the National Park Service.

National Road
The first American highway planned and funded at the federal level, the National Road was legislated by Congress in 1808. It was built from Cumberland, Maryland, in the east (with an extension to Baltimore added during construction) to East St. Louis, Illinois, in the west. Later, when the federal government assigned numbers to interstate highways in the 1920s, the National Road became part of U.S. 40.

Navajo (or Navaho)
1. Currently the largest Native-American tribe. Their reservation lies north of U.S. 66 in northeastern Arizona, northwestern

New Mexico, and southern Utah. They and their unique language served a strategic role in World War II. See CODE TALKERS. 2. A small Route 66 community in Arizona several miles east of Petrified Forest National Park.

Neon

1. A rare, inert gas which glows reddish-orange when exposed to an electrical discharge and is used commercially in illumi-nated signage. 2. Informal: Commercial signage utilizing neon for its illumination, characterized by long, continuous lengths of glass tubing shaped into letters and other graphical elements. This type of sign was in popular use from the 1920s to the 1950s, until it began to be replaced by cheaper technology.

Nicknames

U.S. 66 acquired several nicknames over the years, including Mother Road, Diagonal Highway, Main Street of America (or America's Main Street), and Will Rogers Highway.

Nine-Mile Hill
A hill west of Albuquerque, New Mexico, so named because it is approximately that distance from the city's center.

Nunn's Café
(Shamrock, TX) Former name for what is now the U Drop Inn, a café-gas station enterprise at the junction of U.S. 66 and U.S. 83 in the Texas Panhandle. See U DROP INN.

Nut House
(Claremore, OK) A store specializing in pecans and constructed of pecan logs cut from the surrounding grove. It is very near the Blue Whale of Catoosa and is notable for the odd assortment of antique

vehicles strewn about the grounds, including fire engines, a bus, and a covered wagon. See also BLUE WHALE.

Oak Knoll Manor
(Kirkwood, MO) The housing subdivision that was built on the site of the Coral Court

Motel in suburban St. Louis. The development's entry on Watson Road features the original gates to the motel. See also CORAL COURT MOTEL.

Oak Ridge Cemetery

(Springfield, IL) Large cemetery in the Illinois capital where the city's most famous citizen, President Abraham Lincoln, is interred.

Obelisk

A tall, four-sided tapering shaft of stone that ends in a pointed, pyramid-shaped cap. The most well-known example in the United States is the Washington Monument, located in the District of Columbia. Obelisks were also used to mark certain early U.S. highways. There is an example still standing on an old, disused alignment of U.S. 66/Ozark Trail just to the west of Stroud, Oklahoma.

Odell Standard Station

(Odell, IL) A service station built in the early 1930s that initially sold Standard Oil

products. In 1999, the property was acquired by the city for purposes of restoration. Today, it stands as an excellent example of what such efforts can accomplish.

Odology

The study of roads and motorways. The term was coined by geographer John B. Jackson in the 1980s.

Okie

Nickname—originally pejorative—given to Oklahomans (and other migrants) fleeing their homes during the Dust Bowl years of the Great Depression. Today, the term is used rather freely to refer to Oklahoma natives, with few or no negative connotations.

Old Log Cabin Inn

(Pontiac, IL) This restaurant's claim to fame is that it dealt with the realignment of Route 66 in this area in a unique way—the building was picked up and re-oriented toward the new highway. Today, you can still see the older highway behind the restaurant near the railroad tracks, and that's the direction the building once faced.

Old Town Museum
(Elk City, OK) An expanding complex of vintage buildings (some original, some reproduction) comprising a historical village adjacent to the National Route 66 Mu-

seum. The city was working on this collection even before the 66 museum was conceived, and it includes a gas station, drugstore, tee-pee, caboose, barbershop, water-driven mill, and more.

Our Lady of the Highway
A small shrine near the town of Waggoner, Illinois, to remind travelers of the dangers of highway travel. It was established in 1959 by the Marten family, who still maintain the site. Additionally, there is a series of roadside signs that together comprise the "Hail Mary" prayer, à la Burma Shave. See also BURMA SHAVE.

Owl Court
(Oklahoma City, OK) A small motel court that is located on Route 66's "beltline"

route through the city. The area where the Owl is located—now buried in suburban Oklahoma City—was once the town of Britton. See also BRITTON.

Owl Rock

A rocky outcropping west of Albuquerque, New Mexico (near Mesita), that earned its name from its oddly birdlike silhouette.

Ozark Court

(Stanton, MO) This former motel included a distinctive sign featuring a prancing deer

visible to passing Route 66 travelers long after the motel went out of business; the sign has since been removed.

Ozark Region

Mountainous plateau region of southwestern Missouri and northwestern Arkansas. The Route 66 town of Springfield, Missouri, is nicknamed Queen of the Ozarks. See also GASCOZARK.

Ozark Trail

Actually a *network* of highways—rather than a single route—mostly in Missouri, Oklahoma, Texas, and New Mexico, which predated the numbered Federal Interstate Highway System of 1926. Parts of the Ozark Trail network were superceded by U.S. 66, and there is evidence of this in the form of an Ozark Trail marker (a stone obelisk) still standing just outside the town of Stroud, Oklahoma.

Painted Desert

An expansive swath of hills, mesas, and buttes in northeastern Arizona noted for its brightly hued, arid soil. The area extends from just east of the Grand Canyon eastward to the Petrified Forest. Petrified Forest National Park lies within the Painted Desert.

Painted Desert Inn

A former inn within Petrified Forest National Park that was constructed by Civilian Conservation Corps labor in the

1930s. The building underwent extensive renovations in 2005–'06, and now serves as a museum and bookstore. See also CIVILIAN CONSERVATION CORPS; PETRIFIED FOREST.

Painted Desert Trading Post

A ruinous structure on a long-abandoned section of Route 66 east of Holbrook, Arizona. The ruins are accessible by leaving Interstate 40 at exit #320.

Panhandle

An informal term for a portion of a political territory that protrudes from the main part of the territory in more or less the shape of the

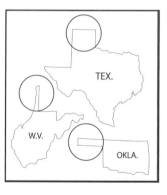

handle on a cooking vessel. Several U.S. states have areas referred to as panhandles; U.S. 66 made its path through Texas entirely within the state's panhandle.

Andy Payne

(1907–1977) Native of Foyil, Oklahoma, who finished as the winner of the Great Transcontinental Foot Race, a publicity event also commonly referred to as the Bunion Derby. There is a sculpture of Mr. Payne on the edge of the town of Foyil alongside old 66. See also BUNION DERBY.

Pecos National Historical Park

(Pecos, NM) A group of historic sites southeast of Santa Fe including the pueblo of Pecos, colonial-era missions, the Civil War Battle of Glorieta Pass, and various Santa Fe Trail sites.

Pecos River

River that arises northwest of Santa Rosa, New Mexico, and empties into the Rio Grande near Del Rio, Texas. The Pecos is referenced fre-

quently in histories of the American West, and indeed the phrase "west of the Pecos" became a synonym for the rugged terrain and rough-and-tumble quality of life in that region.

Marlin Perkins

(1905–1986) A native of Carthage, Missouri, Richard Marlin Perkins worked at both the St. Louis Zoo and the Lincoln Park (Chicago) Zoo before gaining fame as the host of the *Wild Kingdom* television series beginning in the early 1960s. A statue of him stands in Carthage's Central Park.

Petrified Forest

Well-known natural wonder in east-central Arizona, officially Petrified Forest National Park (designated as such in 1962). The park's main attraction is its enormous aggregation of petrified wood—trees that have been fossilized over the eons into mineralized facsimiles of themselves.

Petroglyph

A rock inscription, particularly Native-American artwork. For example, there is a significant collection of petroglyphs arrayed for viewing  at the Petroglyph National Monument on the western outskirts of Albuquerque, New Mexico.

Phillips 66

A brand of gasoline and other automotive products manufactured by Phillips Petroleum of Bartlesville, Oklahoma. The brand uses the number "66" and a highway shield as its logo, which is a close facsimile of the official U.S. 66 road signs of the mid-twentieth century. The story goes that the idea for the name came about when some company officials were out in the field road-testing a new fuel formula. Impressed with the performance of the vehicle on the new fuel, they observed that they were traveling 66 miles per hour on Highway 66 at the time. Notable examples of vintage Phillips 66 stations can be seen today in McLean, Texas, and Chandler, Oklahoma.

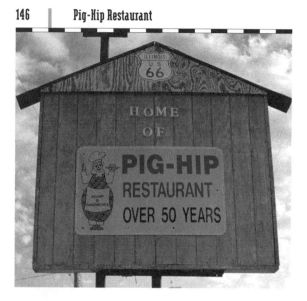

Pig-Hip Restaurant

(Broadwell, IL) Eatery established by Ernie Edwards in 1937 and known for its patented pork sandwiches. The restaurant closed in the 1990s, but was later converted into a museum. Tragically, the building and its contents were consumed by fire in March 2007. Since then, Ernie has been receiving visitors at his home next door, where he has a limited amount of memorabilia to enjoy. As of this writing, what remains of the Pig-Hip legacy may be transferred to The Mill in Lincoln once that structure's restoration is completed and it is reopened as a museum. See also THE MILL.

Pigeon's Ranch

(Glorieta, NM) Stagecoach stop on the Santa Fe Trail that was the scene for some of the fighting in the Battle of Glorieta Pass in the American Civil War.

Pioneer Camp
(Wellston, OK) A for-mer tourist camp on the eastern outskirts of town, the site is currently occupied by a restaurant spe-cializing in barbe-cue. Most notable is a small totem pole whose whimsical figures have beaded  eyes. Also remaining on the property from its days as a tourist camp is a pair of stone foundations, which formed the base for an archway that once spanned the entrance to the compound.

Plateau
An elevated expanse of land, covering a much larger area than a mesa. Route 66 passes across the Ozark Plateau in south-western Missouri. See also MESA.

Pony Truss
See TRUSS BRIDGE.

Pop Hicks Restaurant
(Clinton, OK) Ethan "Pop" Hicks took over

the Bradford Café in 1936 and after a few years changed the name (he was called "Pop" by some of his young waitresses at the time). The restaurant continued to do business for several decades under a variety of ownerships, and achieved landmark status among those in the know. Sadly, a fire claimed the building in 1999, and the restaurant has never reopened. The Oklahoma Route 66 Museum elsewhere in town has information and memorabilia regarding this lost icon.

POPS

(Arcadia, OK) A gas station and soda fountain that opened in the summer of 2007 to considerable fanfare. About 400 varieties of soft drinks are available on premises, and the building is set off by a 66-foot-tall tower in the shape of a pop bottle, which illuminates at night. There is also a collection of more than 12,000 bottles on display inside. The building's architect, Rand Elliott, also designed the Oklahoma Route 66 Museum in Clinton.

Portland Cement
The most common cement, or binder, used in the manufacture of concrete. Portland cement was patented in 1824 by an English engineer, who named it for the limestone cliffs of England's Isle of Portland. See also CONCRETE.

Wiley Post
World-famous aviator who perished with Will Rogers in a plane crash near Point Barrow, Alaska, in 1935. He was a highly accomplished flier, and completed the first successful solo flight around the world in 1933. He is buried in Memorial Park Cemetery on the northern outskirts of Oklahoma City.

Powerhouse Visitors' Center
(Kingman, AZ) Former power-generation facility, and now home to the Historic Route 66 Association of Arizona, a gallery, and a Route 66-themed gift shop. The Powerhouse is a major stop in the annual Route 66 Fun Run, a Mother Road tradition since 1988.

Powers Museum

(Carthage, MO) A museum specializing in local history, the Powers is located on what was formerly the site of Taylor Tourist Park, and later, the Park Motor Court & Café. In keeping with that heritage, in 2005 the museum initiated its "Traveling Classroom Trunks" program for teachers, including one "trunk" with a Highways/Route 66 theme.

Prairie

Derived from the French word for "meadow," prairie refers to land of relatively flat topography that historically supported grasses and few trees. In particular, it refers to that portion of North America often referred to as the Great Plains, characterized by grassy ground cover. In the United States, this includes virtually all of Kansas, Oklahoma, Texas, Nebraska, Wyoming, Colorado, Montana, and the Dakotas, as well as significant portions of Illinois, Indiana, Iowa, Missouri, Wisconsin, and Minnesota. The eastern, or tallgrass, portion has largely been converted to farmland.

Preservation

The act of maintaining (a structure) in an unchanging condition; the prevention of deterioration. This is not synonymous with restoration, though the two are often confused, with the term "preservation" often being used to refer to projects more properly identified as restoration. See also RESTORATION.

Provine

Somewhat arcane name for the U.S. 66 intersection just south of Hydro, Oklahoma, that was the home of Hamon's Courts and later Lucille's. The term is used in the official description of the location  in the National Register of Historic Places.

Quantrill's Raiders

A small, loosely connected group of guerilla raiders under the leadership of William Quantrill during the American Civil War. This pro-Confederacy group was especially active in southwestern Kansas and western Missouri. There is an exhibit pertaining to some of their activities at the Baxter Springs Heritage Center & Museum in Baxter Springs, Kansas.

Queen of the Ozarks
Nickname given to Springfield, Missouri, due to its size and position within the Ozark region of the central U.S.

Radiator Springs
Fictional Route 66 town that was the setting for most of the animated film *Cars*.

Rail Splitter (or Railsplitter)
1. A nickname for Abraham Lincoln, sixteenth president of the United States. 2. Official title of a sculpture of Lincoln, which stands in front of one of the buildings on the Illinois State Fairgrounds in Springfield. The sculpture (completed in 1968) is the work of Carl W. Rinnus, a Springfield native. 3. A greatly oversized figure of Abraham Lincoln driving a covered wagon, which now stands in Lincoln, Illinois. The wagon has been recognized by Guinness as the world's largest at 40 feet (12 meters) in length and weighing in at about 5 tons (4,536 kilograms).

Rainbow Bridge
An arched bridge dating from the 1920s (predating Route 66) that spans Brush Creek west of Riverton, Kansas.

"Rattlesnakes Exit Now"

Well-known sign displayed high above I-40 exhorting travelers to use the next exit in order to experience a reptile display. The aging sign was partially downed by a storm in 2006, and is being repaired for display in nearby McLean, Texas.

Realignment

The act of reassigning the path a highway takes through a given area. This can be done either by diverting traffic along different existing thoroughfares (which often happens within city limits), or by actually building a new roadbed to bear the traffic (common in more rural areas). In either case, the navigational signs used by motorists are relocated.

Vinnie Ream

(1847–1914) Lavinia Ellen Ream was an American sculptor whose most famous work is the figure of President Abraham Lincoln that resides in the U.S. Capitol rotunda. She received that commission from

Congress in 1866, at the tender age of 18. Ream also created a statue of Sequoyah, inventor of the Cherokee alphabet, for the Statuary Hall in the U.S. Capitol. The Route 66 town of Vinita, Oklahoma, was renamed in honor of Vinnie Ream (formerly Downingville).

Red Cedar Inn

(Pacific, MO) Family-run eatery that has been in business since the 1930s, and whose dominant physical feature consists of the hand-cut logs used in its construction.

Red Earth

Describing the state and territory of Oklahoma; the area's soil is very red due to the clay content. Many Oklahoma events and businesses make use of "red earth" in their names.

Red Fork

A small community southwest of Tulsa, Oklahoma. Oil was discovered there in 1901, an event which led to a boom period for Tulsa and the rest of the area.

Red Oak II

A group of old buildings just northeast of

Carthage, Missouri, many of which were moved to this location by artist Lowell Davis, who grew up in the original town of Red Oak.

Red River
River that forms a large part of the border between the states of Oklahoma and Texas. The North Fork of the Red River was the center of a border dispute between the two territories. See also 100TH MERIDIAN.

Red's Giant Hamburg
(Springfield, MO) Restaurant notable for at least two things: the truncated form of its specialty dish, the hamburger; and also for its claim of being the first restaurant to feature drive-thru service, beginning in 1947. Unfortunately for today's hungry Route 66 traveler, Red's was demolished in 1997.

Frank Redford
(?–1958) The originator, in the 1930s, of the Wigwam Village Motel concept. Each "village" was comprised of several discrete motel units, with each unit taking the shape of a Native-American dwelling (most commonly referred to as a "teepee"). At one time, the Wigwam Villages achieved

the status of a small chain scattered across the country, and Mr. Redford collected his franchise fees in an unusual way—each room was equipped with a coin-operated radio, the proceeds of which were forwarded to Mr. Redford. See also WIGWAM VILLAGE.

Lillian Redman

(1909–1999) A former Harvey Girl and longtime proprietress of the Blue Swallow Motel of Tucumcari, New Mexico, Lillian Redman received the motel as an engagement gift in 1958. A beloved friend to all travelers, the following was among her favorite sentiments: "From birth 'til death we travel between the eternities. May these days be pleasant for you, profitable for society, helpful to those you meet, and a joy to those who know and love you best." Mrs. Redman sold the Blue Swallow in 1998 due to failing health after having operated it for forty years. See also HARVEY GIRL; BLUE SWALLOW MOTEL.

Redneck Capital of the World
Self-effacing name given by Harley and Annabelle Russell to their tiny corner of Route 66, the Sandhills Curiosity Shop. See also SANDHILLS CURIOSITY SHOP.

Regal Reptile Ranch
(Alanreed, TX) Long gone, this tourist stop was located on a bypass section of Route 66 on the north edge of town. A large, crudely made snake's  head, which formerly advertised the place, is now part of the collection at the Route 66 Museum in nearby McLean, Texas.

Regionality
The quality of there being discernible differences in language, cuisine, and other cultural expressions from place to place within the same country (or other geopolitical entity). Regionality is becoming a casualty of today's society, due in large part to national-level corporations, brands,

media, and so forth. While some argue that the "shared experience" gained from this trend is valuable, others lament the gradual disappearance of what was once a broad array of cultural manifestations varying from one locality to another.

Rest Haven

Popular and relatively common name for tourist accommodations, bearing the name "camp," "court," or "motel" during the various phases of roadside development. There are two remaining on Route 66: a still-operating motel in Springfield, Missouri, and a defunct one in Afton, Oklahoma, which still has a standing sign.

Restoration

The bringing back of a building or other structure to its original (or near-original) condition. Often, people use the term "preservation" when in fact they are referring to restoration. See also PRESERVATION.

Rialto Square Theatre

(Joliet, IL) A truly sumptuous theater, which

was built in 1925 and celebrated its opening May 24, 1926, the Rialto early on attained unofficial status as the "Jewel of Joliet." The theater's decor includes bas-reliefs depicting scenes from classical

mythology, as well as a lobby area modeled after the Hall of Mirrors at the world-renowned Palace of Versailles.

Lynn Riggs

(1899–1954) Oklahoma-born playwright whose 1931 play *Green Grow the Lilacs* formed the basis of the well-known Rodgers and Hammerstein musical production, *Oklahoma!* The Lynn Riggs Memorial is a small museum dedicated to his life and career in Claremore, Oklahoma. See also GREEN GROW THE LILACS.

Right-of-Way

The strip of land granted by a governing authority for the establishment of railways. Subsequently, due to the facilitating presence of the railway, it was along these same rights-of-way that power lines and highways were constructed in close proximity.

Rimmy Jim

Rimmy Jim Giddings operated a small trading post about 40 miles east of Flagstaff,

Arizona. Today, the I-40 exit number 233 is labeled "Rimmy Jims" on many maps. It's at that particular exit (Meteor Crater Road) that one can see what remains of another of Rimmy Jim's ventures: Meteor Crater Observatory. A stone tower and museum were constructed there in the 1930s when Route 66 passed right at its doorstep. It fell into disuse when the highway was realigned a little to the north about 1949.

Rio Grande

River that today forms the border between Mexico and the U.S. state of Texas. At the time Texas seceded from Mexico (1836), it claimed

the Rio Grande as its western border near Albuquerque and Santa Fe. (Spanish: *rio* = river + *grande* = large)

Jack D. Rittenhouse

Author of *A Guide Book to Highway 66*, published in 1946. Mr. Rittenhouse foresaw that the post-World War II years would be marked by an increase in western highway travel, and so in March of 1946 he traveled the length of Route 66 jotting down every possible detail for his self-published book. His guide includes city population figures, historical sites, mileages between towns, and such essentials as availability of food, fuel, lodging, and automotive repair. A facsimile edition of the *Guide Book* was published by New Mexico University Press in 1989.

Riviera Roadhouse

(Gardner, IL) Dating from the 1920s—and Prohibition—the Riviera is reputed to have been a hangout for gangsters, including Al Capone, during its early days. Behind the main building is a restored horse-drawn streetcar, a project of the Preservation Committee of the Route 66 Association of Illinois. See also ROADHOUSE.

Road Warrior

1. (lower case) A road-trip enthusiast, or

roadie. See also ROADIE. 2. (upper case) A student or alumnus of Route 66 University.

Roadhouse

An establishment that serves meals and has a bar serving beer or spirits, and which commonly features music for entertainment. Most roadhouses are located along highways in rural areas or on the outskirts of towns. Early on, roadhouses typically offered rooms for the night as well, but this became far less common coincident with the rise of motels after World War II.

Roadie

A person who is enthusiastic about—and frequently indulges in—automobile trips in which the destination is often secondary to the experience of the journey itself. Top-tier roadies are adventurous enough to embrace new experiences, wrong turns, and even unexpected difficulties in their pursuit of road-trip nirvana.

Rock Café

(Stroud, OK) Restaurant dating from 1939 and constructed from native stone unearthed during the excavation and paving of Route 66 through the area. The café's owner, Dawn Welch, was the primary inspiration for the character of Sally the Porsche in the Route 66-themed movie *Cars*.

Will Rogers

(1879–1935) William Penn Adair Rogers was an internationally known humorist, movie actor, and social commentator who had close ties to Route 66. He was born near Oologah, Indian Territory (now Oklahoma) from parents of Cherokee heritage. He purchased property in the Route 66 city of Claremore, Oklahoma, which he intended one day to be his retirement home; that property is now the location of the Will Rogers Memorial and the family tomb. Will Rogers World Airport in Oklahoma City was named for him, as was the Will Rogers Turnpike, a section of Interstate 44 northeast of Tulsa. He lived his last several years just northwest of Santa Monica,

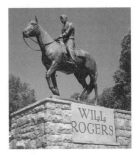

California, at what is now Will Rogers State Historic Park. In 1952, as part of promotion for a motion picture based on Rogers' life, the majority of Route 66 was quasi-officially nicknamed the Will Rogers Highway. Several plaques were placed along the route at that time, one of which can still be seen in Santa Monica, near the highway's western terminus. It reads, in part, "Highway 66 was the first road he traveled in a career that led him straight to the hearts of his countrymen."

George and Melba Rook

It was at George and Melba's store at Landergin, Texas, in 1996 that the National Historic Route 66 Federation held its first-ever national-level festival, called Run to the Heartland. George was one of the early presidents of the Old Route 66 Association of Texas, and, beginning in the early 1990s, was the driving force behind getting "Historic Route 66" signs added to key I-40 exit signs in the state. George has since passed away, but Melba lives on in the panhandle town of Spearman, Texas. See also RUN TO THE HEARTLAND.

Jim Ross

Author of the thoroughly researched guide to Oklahoma's portion of the Mother Road, *Oklahoma Route 66*, and co-creator of the

Here It Is! series of Route 66 maps. Jim was the recipient of the John Steinbeck Award in 2001 and is also a member of the Oklahoma Route 66 Hall of Fame. Also notable is his home in Arcadia, Oklahoma, the façade of which resembles a vintage Phillips 66 cottage-style station. See also JOHN STEINBECK AWARD; COTTAGE-STYLE.

Rotosphere
A sphere-shaped object that revolves along its vertical axis, and which is also split so as to allow the two hemispheres to rotate in opposing directions. The sign at the El Comedor de Anayas restaurant in Moriarty, New Mexico, includes a rotosphere in its design. That sign was restored as part of a statewide program, and is now the only fully operational rotosphere on Route 66.

Round Barn
(Arcadia, OK) Built in 1898, this barn with a circular floor plan sits alongside Route 66

and was fully restored and rehabilitated in the 1990s. There is now a gift shop inside to welcome Mother Road travelers.

Route

1. A physical pathway for travel from one place to another. 2. A common way of referring to numbered highways in the United States; e.g., "Route 66" has become the most common way of referring to U.S. 66.

Route 66

1. See chapter entitled "A Short Introduction to Route 66" at the beginning of this book. 2. The name of a song composed by Bobby Troup in 1946, more commonly known by its unofficial title, "(Get Your Kicks on) Route 66." The song has been recorded by many, many artists over the years from a variety of musical genres. 3. A television series that aired in the early 1960s. See also *ROUTE 66* TELEVISION SERIES.

Route 66 Associations

Each of the eight states through which Route 66 passed has at least one nonprofit organization set up to preserve, promote, and otherwise support the highway and

its businesses. Credit is often given to Angel Delgadillo for instigating the first of
these groups, the Historic Route 66 Association of Arizona, which was established
in 1987, just a few scant years after U.S.
66 had been completely bypassed by the
Interstate Highway System. See also ANGEL
DELGADILLO.

Route 66 Caravan
A caravan sponsored by Hampton Hotels'
Save-A-Landmark program, held in 2003,
in which "Route 66 Roadside Attraction"
signs were presented and posted at numerous iconic locations along Route 66. See
also SAVE-A-LANDMARK.

Route 66 Corridor Preservation Program
From the organization's mission statement:
"The National Park Service Route 66 Corridor Preservation Program collaborates
with partners to provide funding, techni-
cal assistance, and education towards the
long-term preservation of the most repre-
sentative and significant resources of the
historic Route 66 corridor."

Route 66 Magazine
Full-color quarterly periodical dedicated
entirely to U.S. 66 and published since
1994.

Route 66 Preservation Foundation

Formerly the California Route 66 Preservation Foundation, the group later broadened its focus and altered its name. According to the official website: "The goal of the Route 66 Preservation Foundation is to raise the positive visibility of Route 66 among a variety of audiences, including the general public." The foundation now recognizes significant Route 66 personages through several awards, including the Will Rogers Award. See also WILL ROGERS AWARD.

Route 66 Pulse

Near-monthly newspaper dedicated entirely to feature stories and current events pertaining to U.S. 66; first published in 2006.

Route 66 State Park

(Eureka, MO) The park's address is Eureka, but it's actually situated on what was once the community of Times Beach. Times Beach was started in the 1920s as a resort and/or bedroom community for St. Louis, it being just far enough away to be considered rural. Unfortunately, residents learned that during the 1970s the recycled oil sprayed on their streets for dust control was highly contaminated with dioxins. The community was evacuated in the 1980s, later to be cleaned up and converted to the park you see today. The park's main interpretive center is in a building that formerly served as a roadhouse named the Bridgehead Inn, dating from 1935.

Route 66 Television Series

From 1960 to 1964, this television series was shot "on location" throughout the United States and Canada. Although only a small minority of the more than 100 episodes were filmed on the true U.S. 66, the series is renowned for its gritty realism and its sometimes dark plots, which were innovative for their time. The show starred Martin Milner, George Maharis (replaced in later episodes by Glenn Corbett), and a Chevrolet Corvette. See also the "Need to Know More?" section.

Roy Rogers Museum

For decades, the museum honoring the "King of the Cowboys" could be found in the town of Victorville, California (Roy and his wife, Dale Evans, lived nearby in their later years). In 2003, however, the museum's collection was moved to Branson, Missouri, by the surviving family and subsequently renamed the Roy Rogers-Dale Evans Museum. In front of the museum stood a rearing statue of Roy's horse Trigger, which appears to have been the inspiration for the sign for the nearby New Corral Motel.

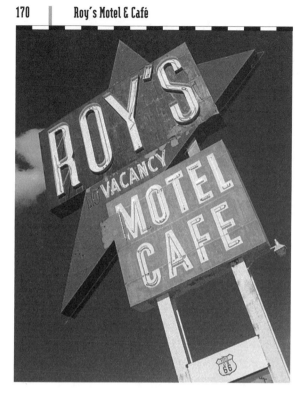

Roy's Motel & Café

(Amboy, CA) A Route 66 tourist complex in the Southern California desert consisting of a motel, café, fuel station, and garage. The complex was built in phases during the 1920s through 1950s. The large sign is a favorite photo opportunity, and dates from approximately 1959.

Run to the Heartland

A Route 66 commemorative festival held in Landergin,

Texas, in 1996; occasion of the presentation of the first John Steinbeck Award to author Michael Wallis. Landergin was selected in large part due to its location at the approximate halfway point of U.S. 66.

Sanders Camera Shop
(Edmond, OK) Notable for occupying a building that once housed the first schoolhouse in Oklahoma Territory.

Sandhills Curiosity Shop
(Erick, OK) Located in a former meat market building in downtown Erick, the Sandhills Curiosity Shop is an unlikely center of entertainment for this small town. The shop is run by Harley and Annabelle Russell, also known as the Mediocre Music Makers. See also MEDIOCRE MUSIC MAKERS.

Santa Fe Trail
A significant trade route for much of the

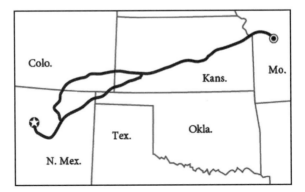

nineteenth century, the trail began in Missouri and ended in Santa Fe, which at the time was in newly independent Mexico. An early alignment of Route 66 closely approximates the Santa Fe Trail from Romeroville, New Mexico, toward Santa Fe. In fact, as that alignment of 66 enters the Santa Fe city limits, the road is named Old Santa Fe Trail.

Save-A-Landmark

Program sponsored by Hampton Hotels in which company volunteers help to recognize and refurbish some of America's noteworthy roadside attractions. The program was initiated in 2000. See also ROUTE 66 CARAVAN.

Scenic Byway

An American road designated as outstanding by the Federal Highway Administration for its historical, cultural, recreational, or other qualities. The National Scenic Byways program was established in 1991 under the Intermodal Surface Transportation Efficiency Act (ISTEA), and highways are nominated on a local, grassroots level.

To date, Historic Route 66 has been designated a National Scenic Byway in Illinois, New Mexico, and Arizona.

Seaba Station
(Warwick, OK) Brick building that served duty on Route 66 both as a NevrNox gasoline station and as an engine-rebuilding shop, and named for its owner, John Seaba.

Second City
1. A nickname for Chicago. 2. The name given to a comedy troupe in the same city from which arose several players who achieved greater fame as members of the *Saturday Night Live* cast.

Sequoyah
Town in northeastern Oklahoma that was named after the Cherokee of the same name (also known as George Guess), who developed an alphabet of the Cherokee language (or more properly, a syllabary).

Shea's
(Springfield, IL) Former fueling station on Route 66 (Peoria Avenue) now housing an extensive collection of gas station-

and Mother Road-related memorabilia. Bill Shea has spent most of his life at the side of the highway, and his one-of-a-kind collection clearly demonstrates it.

Shoe Tree

A tree just east of Stroud, Oklahoma, festooned with several shoes hanging from its branches.

Shunpiker

One who deliberately shuns the larger highways and turnpikes and enjoys using the smaller, more intimate roads.

Sidewalk Highway

In northeastern Oklahoma there are two unique fragments of old U.S. 66 sometimes referred to as the sidewalk highway. This is because they were constructed only about nine feet in width, which is essentially a single lane. The story goes that money was tight, and so the idea was hatched that twice the distance could be paved if it were done at one-half the standard width. This of course necessitated that drivers keep only two of four wheels on the pavement when encountering traffic moving in the opposing direction. These fragments were bypassed fairly early on (1930s), and are still in reasonably good condition. One segment is located to the south side of Miami, Oklahoma, while the other is a little north and east of Afton, Oklahoma.

Sirup

Idiosyncratic spelling of "syrup" used by the Funk family of Illinois to describe their maple product. You can still visit their store and grove of maples near the village of Funk's Grove, Illinois.

Six-Shooter Siding

A former name for Tucumcari, New Mexico.

Sixth Avenue

(Amarillo, TX) Part of Route 66's early alignment through Amarillo passed along Sixth Avenue. This portion of the Route has since been the scene of significant redevelopment, with a number of active businesses both new and old. Sixth Avenue also was the scene of a major Mother Road festival in 1998.

Sky City

Nickname for the Acoma Pueblo, a Native-American village constructed atop a 350-foot-high mesa several miles south of Route 66 in western New Mexico. Inhabitants of Acoma claim that theirs is the oldest continuously inhabited city in the United States.

Smiling Fat Man

(Santa Rosa, NM) Logo for the now-defunct Club Café. It was used on Club Café advertising billboards for many years on Route 66. The smiling fat man has since been incorporated into some of the signage for Joseph's Bar & Grill, also in Santa Rosa.

Snake Pit

Common name given to road-side attractions featuring reptiles of one kind

or another, especially snakes. Synonyms include reptile farm, snake farm, reptile pit, reptile ranch, etc.

Snortin' Norton

Name of the camel mascot for the Campbell's 66 Express trucking company, and whose image appeared on the company's truck trailers with the slogan "Humpin' to Please." A collection of items related to this company and its graphics can be seen at Henry's Rabbit Ranch in Staunton, Illinois. See also HUMPIN' TO PLEASE; HENRY'S RABBIT RANCH.

Snow Cap Drive-In

(Seligman, AZ) Restaurant owned and operated for 50 years by Juan Delgadillo and steeped in Juan's odd brand of humor. A prominent sign on the exterior boasts of "Dead Chicken" as a staple of the menu, and the entry door has multiple handles, only one of which is functional. Juan built the Snow Cap in 1953 from scrap lumber he'd been scrounging while working for the railroad. The Snow Cap continues to

be run by the next generation of Delgadillos since Juan's passing in 2004. A visitor to the Snow Cap can spend considerable time just exploring the grounds, as it is festooned with a variety of signs, props, vintage vehicles, and other trappings. See also JUAN DELGADILLO.

Sooner
Nickname given to citizens of Oklahoma (the Sooner State); it originates from the former Indian Territory's settlement by white homesteaders in the land rushes of 1889, at which time many of the settlers rushed into the territory "sooner" than officials intended.

Soulsby Shell Station
(Mt. Olive, IL) Restored gasoline station that originally opened in 1926, the same

year Route 66 and the rest of the numbered system of interstate highways was certified. The building was constructed by Henry Soulsby and his son Russell, and was actively used in various businesses by the family until the late 1990s, when the property was sold. In 2004, it was added to the National Register of Historic Places.

Spring Tank
An early name for the Texas Panhandle community of Alanreed.

Thomas P. Stafford
A native of the Route 66 town of Weatherford, Oklahoma, where there is today a museum dedicated to his career as an astronaut.

Standard Addition
(Carlinville, IL) Located on an older alignment of Route 66 (Illinois 4), Carlinville is sometimes ignored by Mother Road travelers short on time. But Carlinville has its own treasured piece of Americana—it's the site of the largest single grouping of Sears

Roebuck catalog-order houses in the world. The Standard Addition is an entire company neighborhood (created by Standard Oil) for which they ordered more than 150 houses from Sears and had them  erected here for their employees.

Standin' on a Corner

A sculpture in Winslow, Arizona, capitalizing on a line from the song "Take It Easy," which was written by Jackson Browne and Glenn Frey and popularized by The Eagles in the 1970s: "Standin' on a corner in Winslow, Arizona . . ." The sculpture has become a popular photo opportunity for Mother Road travelers.

John Steinbeck
(1902–1968) Pulitzer Prize-winning author who coined the term "Mother Road" as a reference to Route 66 in his signature novel *The Grapes of Wrath*. See also JOHN STEINBECK AWARD; *THE GRAPES OF WRATH*.

Stonehenge Replica
Stonehenge is a group of standing stones on the Salisbury Plain of southern England, a half-sized replica of which can be found on the campus of the University of Missouri at Rolla. The original Stonehenge is thought to have been an ancient observatory for the motions of the moon and sun.

Streamline Moderne
An architectural style popular in the 1930s, Streamline Moderne was an offshoot of Art Deco emphasizing curving, streamlined shapes, and which often incorporated nautical details such as porthole windows. Examples include the 66 Diner in Albuquerque, New Mexico, and Barnum Hall in Santa Monica, California.

Summit Inn
(Cajon Summit, CA) Café that stands near the crest of Cajon Pass, a mountainous stretch of U.S. 66/I-15 north of San Bernardino. Notably, it features a rare form of

coin-operated fortune-telling napkin holder very similar to that used in a famous episode of *The Twilight Zone* (entitled "Nick of Time"), which starred a young William Shatner.

Superslab
Sometimes-disparaging name for a U.S. interstate highway.

Switchback
A sharp bend in a road on a steep incline. Switchbacks allow the road to climb to a

summit more gradually than a straight approach would. There are numerous switchbacks on the section of old Route 66 between Kingman and Oatman, Arizona.

"Takhomasak"

Promotional "slogan" for Steak 'n Shake restaurants, from "Take Home a Sack[ful]." The restaurant chain also uses "In sight it must be right." There is a Steak 'n Shake on Route 66 in Springfield, Missouri, that is still housed in its original 1962 architecture.

Tarmac

See MACADAM.

Michael Taylor

Director of the National Park Service's Route 66 Corridor Preservation Program, instituted in 1999 and with offices in Santa Fe, New Mexico. The program provides grants to individuals preserving and renovating important Route 66 properties.

Tom Teague

(1943–2004) Founding member and first president of the Route 66 Association of Illinois, Tom was an avid respecter and promoter of all things Route 66. He was the author of *Searching for 66*, a collection of vignettes about the people he met on his Mother Road explorations, and he founded the Soulsby Station Society of Mount Olive to fund the restoration of Illinois's oldest gas station still standing on Route 66. Tom was honored for his many accomplishments in 1998 as recipient of the prestigious John Steinbeck Award. See also JOHN STEINBECK AWARD.

Ted Drewes Frozen Custard

(St. Louis, MO) Since 1930, the Drewes family has been offering their frozen custard confections to St. Louisans at just a handful of loca-

tions. The Route 66 location, on Chippewa, opened in 1941. The specialty of the house is the "concrete," served so thick that it can be turned upside down with nary a drip or spill. See also CONCRETE.

Teepee (or Tepee)

Traditional Native-American dwelling of the Great Plains region constructed of a skeleton of wooden poles bound together at the top, with a broad base, and wrapped in animal hides. On Route 66, a great num-

ber of roadside businesses sought to thematically evoke the Wild West by using the teepee motif in name, construction, and/or decor. The best existing examples are the Wigwam Village Motels and Teepee Curios. See also TEEPEE CURIOS; WIGWAM VILLAGE.

Teepee Curios

(Tucumcari, NM) Occupying a building that was originally constructed as a fuel station in the 1940s, Teepee Curios is one of the best examples of the kitschy ex-

uberance that once typified highwayside commercial architecture in that era. The main entrance is designed to resemble a Native-American teepee.

Terminus

The end of a highway, at which point official markings cease; for example, the eastern terminus of U.S. 66 was in downtown Chicago, Illinois.

Tijeras Canyon
A natural pass just east of Albuquerque, New Mexico, connecting the Rio Grande Valley with the eastern part of the state.

Times Beach
The name of a former community west of St. Louis no longer to be found on maps. For the story, see ROUTE 66 STATE PARK.

Tinkertown Museum
(Sandia Park, NM) East of Albuquerque and just off Route 66 is this family-owned theme park known popularly as Tinkertown. Tinkertown is the labor of love of one man, Ross Ward, who for decades carved and whittled and assembled Tinkertown out of the materials at hand. The main building itself is built largely of thousands of bottles held together with mortar, and inside are literally thousands of hand-carved models and dioramas depicting everything from circuses to ragtime bands to the afterlife, many of which are animated. A sign painter by profes-

sion, Mr. Ward also sprinkled the grounds of Tinkertown liberally with gems of wisdom from such minds as Mark Twain, Teddy Roosevelt, and Will Rogers. But perhaps the pithiest of them all was coined by Ward himself: "I did all this while you were watching TV."

Top Hat Dairy Bar

(Foyil, OK) Small corner store on Route 66 at the junction with Oklahoma State Highway 28A; notable as a landmark for the turn-off to Ed Galloway's iconic Totem Pole Park. See TOTEM POLE PARK.

Top o' the World

A bygone tourist complex in New Mexico, so named because it was located at one of the highest points on Route 66, where the highway crossed the Continental Divide. See CONTINENTAL DIVIDE.

Totem Pole Park

(Foyil, OK) Nathan "Ed" Galloway began constructing what is today known as Totem Pole Park in the 1930s, when he and his wife first took residence at this property in northeastern Oklahoma. He completed their stone residence in 1937, and then began working on an array of Native-Amer-

ican-inspired structures, the most monumental of which is a 90-foot totem pole completed in 1948. Also on the property is an eleven-sided building Ed constructed in order to house his collection of handmade fiddles. Totem Pole Park is today under the custodianship of the Rogers County Historical Society.

Tourist Court
Early term for roadside lodging that eventually evolved into "motel." See MOTEL.

Tourist Trap
A general term for any roadside business that seeks to make its profits through frivolous means, either by offering admission to exhibits of dubious value, or by selling cheap souvenirs and trinkets.

Trade Winds Motel
(Clinton, OK) The Trade Winds stands on Gary Boulevard, a later alignment of Route

66 that skirted the periphery of town. This motel's claim to fame stems from its having hosted Elvis Presley a number of times in room 215 on several of his trips between Tennessee and California.

Trading Post
While the term "trading post" has come to be used to describe almost any retail store, traditionally it refers to a store or station where local barterers would come to exchange handmade goods for needed supplies. Those handmade goods would in turn be sold by the trading post's proprietors to anyone passing through—highway tourists, for example.

Trail of Tears
A forced march, in the 1830s, when the Cherokee people were forced out of their ancestral lands in Georgia, Alabama, Tennessee, and North Carolina by the U.S. government and removed to Tahlequah,

Oklahoma. Although circuitous, one of the routes taken during that march closely approximates the path of Route 66 in central and southwestern Missouri. That segment begins roughly at Rolla, and continues until U.S. 66 leaves the state near the Kansas and Oklahoma borders.

Traveler's Repose
Former name for the Route 66 community of St. Clair, Missouri.

Delbert and Ruth Trew
The Trews live on a ranch near Alanreed, Texas, and a section of an early alignment of Route 66 serves as part of their driveway. They started the Devil's Rope Museum in McLean, Texas, and later added a separate area for Route 66 artifacts. With a grand opening in March of 1991, it became the very first museum dedicated to Route 66. Delbert is a prolific writer on a variety of topics, and Ruth still produces the quarterly newsletter for the Old Route 66 Association of Texas. In 2006, Delbert and Ruth were the recipients of the Lifetime Achievement Award presented by the Route 66 Preservation Foundation. See also DEVIL'S ROPE; ROUTE 66 PRESERVATION FOUNDATION.

Tri-County Truck Stop
(Villa Ridge, MO) A large restaurant sited

where an earlier restaurant had burned. See THE DIAMONDS.

Triangle Motel

(Amarillo, TX) A 1940s-era motel on Amarillo's east side on a relatively obscure section of old 66 (Triangle Drive). In 2007, a preservation effort was launched to preserve the motel.

The Tropics

(Lincoln, IL) Dining room and cocktail lounge whose name was inspired by the owner's service

in Hawaii during World War II. It still sports an excellent neon sign.

Bobby Troup

(1918–1999) American actor, musician, and songwriter whose most famous composition was his song "(Get Your Kicks on) Route 66," originally recorded and popularized by the Nat King Cole Trio. The song was composed in 1946, just after the conclusion of World War II, during a cross-country automobile trip, and was recorded by Nat King Cole later that year. Troup also gained a measure of fame later in life for his portrayal of the Dr. Joe Early character in the 1970s television series *Emergency!*, which also costarred his wife, Julie London.

Truss Bridge (Deck, Through, Pony)

A bridge supported by a framework of beams or struts forming a rigid structure. There are three major types of truss bridge: the deck truss, in which the truss is below the level of the roadway; the through truss, in which the roadway passes direct-

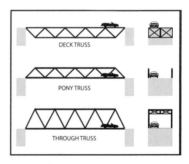

ly through the middle of the truss; and the pony truss, in which the truss extends above but not completely around the roadway (also called a half-through truss).

Tulsey Town

Former name for Tulsa, Oklahoma during its Indian Territory period (prior to statehood). The name is derived from *tulasi*, a Native-American expression of obscure meaning.

Twin Arrows

1. A combination café, trading post, and gas station east of Winona, Arizona, featuring two greatly oversized arrows angling into the ground. 2. An exit from I-40 by the same name.

Two Guns

Site of an early trading post and a later tourist-trap complex where Route 66 crossed the Canyon Diablo in Arizona. It lies about 20–25 miles west of the

town of Winslow. The property is usually closed to the public.

U Drop Inn

(Shamrock, TX) Formerly called Nunn's Café, the U Drop Inn is a combination gas

station and café complex situated on Route 66 where it crosses U.S. 83 in the Texas Panhandle. The building, in the Art Deco style, was conceived in the 1920s by John Nunn, who is said to have sketched the original design in the Texas soil using a nail. In 2003, the building was beautifully restored and has since become the home of the local chamber of commerce. See also NUNN'S CAFÉ.

Ugly Crust Pies

A specialty of the house at the Midpoint Café in Adrian, Texas. Joann Harwell, long-time baker at the café, nicknamed them as such because she couldn't seem to get the knack for making her crusts look quite as presentable as the ones she remembered her grandmother making.

Valentine

1. A town in northwestern Arizona on Route 66. 2. A manufacturer of diners based in Wichita, Kansas, and operating from the late 1930s until the mid-1970s. The restored diner on display on the grounds of the Oklahoma Route 66 Museum in Clinton, Oklahoma, was manufactured by Valentine.

Wagon Wheel Motel

(Cuba, MO) An old, well-kept motel that still offers today's traveler a taste of what the simple accommodations of yesteryear were like. The motel also features a unique sign in fine condition that includes a neon-trimmed wagon wheel.

Ed Waldmire, Jr.

Purported inventor of the battered and deep-fried hot dog on a stick, and founder of the Cozy Dog Drive-In of Springfield, Illinois, for which his own version of the treat is named. One of Ed Waldmire's sons, Bob, is a well-known artist whose favorite subjects include every imaginable Route 66 structure or attraction. See also COZY DOG; ROBERT "BOB" WALDMIRE.

Robert "Bob" Waldmire

The son of Cozy Dog founder Ed Waldmire, Jr., Bob Waldmire is an accomplished art-

ist well known for his pen-and-ink drawings specializing in wildlife and Route 66 sites. Bob's lifestyle is as "off-the-grid" as he can manage it, as evidenced by his isolated residential compound in southeastern Arizona. In 2004, Bob was honored for his efforts on behalf of Route 66 as recipient of the John Steinbeck Award. See also JOHN STEINBECK AWARD.

Michael Wallis

A prolific author and popular speaker, Wallis' book *Route 66: The Mother Road* is widely credited with launching the resurgence in interest in Route 66 during the 1990s. In 1996, he became the first recipient of the John Steinbeck Award, presented by the National Historic Route 66 Federation. Wallis also was the chief consultant to the production team responsible for creating the animated film *Cars*. The movie, which is set in a fictional town on Route 66, was released in 2006 and features Michael's distinctive voice as the character of the sheriff.

John and Lenore Weiss

The Weisses have tirelessly worked to preserve numerous Route 66 sites in their home state of Illinois, and their names are virtually synonymous with the Route 66 Association of Illinois's Preservation Committee. In 2002, they were honored with the John Steinbeck Award (the only couple to ever receive it).

White Fence Farm
(Romeoville, IL) A large dining complex specializing in chicken dinners that dates from the 1920s. There is a large, attention-getting fiberglass chicken by the highwayside, and the grounds also include a petting zoo, antique car museum, and several other tourable collections.

Whiting Brothers
Now-defunct roadside services chain that at

one time was prominent in the American Southwest, including U.S. 66. Though some were gasoline stations only, many were complexes that included lodgings, cafés, and general stores as well.

Whiz Kids
The Baxter Springs Whiz Kids semiprofessional baseball team roster once boasted future legend Mickey Mantle. It was while playing for the Whiz Kids in the late 1940s that Mickey was "discovered" by a scout for the New York Yankees. Mantle had

close ties with Route 66 towns: not only did he play ball in Baxter Springs, Kansas, he grew up a little further down the highway in Commerce, Oklahoma.

Whoopee Coaster

(McCook, IL) An amusement ride that operated in the 1920s near the intersection of Joliet Road and Lawndale Avenue. It was similar to a roller coaster, with the difference being that the patrons rode the hilly wooden track in their own vehicles. In subsequent years, however, personal automobiles became wider and heavier, and the needed modification and upkeep of the track became impractical.

Wigwam Village

 Any one of several motels in the U.S. that were part of a small chain with individual rooms built to resemble Native-American traditional dwellings (more properly called tee-pees). Of the total, two were (and are) on Route 66: one in Holbrook, Arizona, and another in Rialto, California. The ownership of the Wigwam Village Motel in California was recognized

with the Cyrus Avery preservation award in 2005 for their complete refurbishment of the motel.

Will Rogers Award

Beginning in 2006, this award has been presented to an individual who has had a significant impact on the continuation of Route 66. The inaugural award in 2006 went to John Lasseter, producer of the animated film *Cars*, which was released that year. In 2007, the award was presented to author Michael Wallis. See also JOHN LASSETER; *CARS*; MICHAEL WALLIS.

Will Rogers Highway

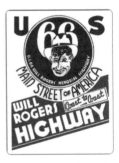

One of several nicknames for U.S. 66. Although there were some efforts to name Route 66 after Will Rogers shortly after his death in 1935, it was in 1952 that the moniker became semi-official. Warner Bros., as part of promotion for a soon-to-be-released film called *The Story of Will Rogers*, sponsored a caravan along the length of U.S. 66 and placed several commemorative plaques, one of which can be seen in Palisades Park, near the highway's western end in Santa Monica, California. See also WILL ROGERS; NICKNAMES.

Will Rogers Memorial

(Claremore, OK) Museum and final resting place of humorist Will Rogers. The property was originally intended by Rogers to be his retirement home once his Hollywood career had come to an end. See WILL ROGERS.

Works Progress Administration (WPA)

An agency of the U.S. government created in 1935, during the height of the Great Depression, to provide work for the unemployed. During eight years of existence, the WPA employed millions of workers and built hundreds of thousands of miles of roads, as well as thousands of public buildings and bridges.

World's Largest Catsup Bottle

(Collinsville, IL) This 170-foot-tall water tower was built in 1949 outside the bottling plant for Brooks Catsup. It's composed of a 70-foot-tall catsup-bottle-shaped tank on top of a 100-foot-tall steel base. In 1995, a concerned group of citizens restored it to its original appearance, and it is now listed on the National Register of Historic Places. Although many people prefer the "ketchup" spelling, "catsup" is used on the official website and other materials. See also the "Need to Know More?" section.

Frank Lloyd Wright

(1867–1959) American architect known for developing his "prairie style" of architectural design and for having achieved significant fame and notoriety even during his lifetime—a rare achievement. His studio was located in Oak Park, Illinois (greater Chicago), where there is a large concentration of residences he designed, and there are quite a number of buildings of his design still standing in several Route 66 cities, including Dwight and Springfield, Illinois, and Tulsa, Oklahoma.

Wrink's Food Market

(Lebanon, MO) A small neighborhood store on Route 66 that was operated continuously for over 50 years by Glenn Wrinkle. After his death in 2005, the store was shuttered for about two years un-

til his son Terry reopened it in July 2007. The store achieved a measure of fame when its 99-cent bologna sandwich was recommended by Paul Harvey on his nationwide radio program in the early 1990s. See also GLENN WRINKLE.

Glenn Wrinkle

(1923–2005) Glenn "Wrink" Wrinkle owned and operated Wrink's Food Market on Route 66 in Lebanon, Missouri, from 1950 until just a few weeks before  his death. Because of his innately generous soul, Wrink died a rich man—leaving behind more devoted friends than he could count. In 2007, more than two years after his death, W.R. Case & Sons Cutlery produced a limited-edition commemorative knife in Wrink's honor. See also WRINK'S FOOD MARKET.

Xenia

Former name for the city of Atlanta, Illinois. Atlanta is known today for being the home of the muffler man relocated from Bunyon's restaurant in Cicero (suburban Chicago). See also MUFFLER MAN; BUNYON'S.

Yukon Motel

(Yukon, OK) A motel that once had a tall, impressive neon sign out front dating from the late 1950s. Inexplicably, although it still operates as a motel, a change in ownership in 2001 resulted in the sign's being taken down and replaced by something utterly nondescript and without character. Many Route 66 aficionados are still scratching their heads.

Yukon's Best

A brand of flour with headquarters in Yukon, Oklahoma; the company name is emblazoned on a set of grain elevators alongside Route 66 in the center of town. The city of Yukon bills itself as the "Czech Capital of Oklahoma."

Zella's Café

(Adrian, TX) Café formerly doing business in the building now occupied by the Midpoint Café. See also MIDPOINT CAFÉ.

Zuni

A Native-American tribe of the southwestern United States known for their distinctive pottery. The Zuni Pueblo (or village) is about 35 miles south of Gallup, New Mexico.

Need to Know More?

Burma Shave
For the detailed story of Burma Shave and its unique roadside form of advertising, including reprints of all 600 original rhymes, see:

Rowsome, Frank, Jr. *The Verse by the Side of the Road: The Story of the Burma-Shave Signs and Jingles*. Brattleboro, VT: Stephen Greene Press, 1965.

Coral Court Motel
For the definitive story behind one of the most renowned motels on all of 66:

Graham, Shellee. *Tales from the Coral Court: Photos and Stories from a Lost Route 66 Landmark*. St. Louis, MO: Virginia Publishing, 2000.

History of Route 66
For a detailed treatment of the genesis of U.S. 66:

Kelly, Susan Croce, and Quinta Scott. *Route 66: The Highway and Its People*. Norman, OK: University of Oklahoma Press, 1988.

Lincoln Highway
Entire books have been written about Route 66's best-known sibling:

Butko, Brian. *Greetings from the Lincoln Highway: America's First Coast-to-Coast Road*. Mechanicsburg, PA: Stackpole Books, 2005.

Wallis, Michael, and Michael J. Williamson. *The Lincoln Highway: Coast to Coast from Times Square to the Golden Gate*. New York: W. W. Norton & Co., 2007.

Maps & Guides

The following are invaluable for a detailed exploration of Route 66. Some specialize in certain areas, while some cover the highway in its entirety:

Clark, David G. *Exploring Route 66 in Chicagoland: Journeys Through History on the Mother Road in Cook County, Illinois*. Chicago, IL: WindyCityRoad Warrior.com, 2006.

Knowles, Drew. *Route 66 Adventure Handbook*. Santa Monica, CA: Santa Monica Press, 2006.

Mangum, Richard and Sherry. *Route 66 Across Arizona: A Comprehensive Two-Way Guide for Touring Route 66*. Flagstaff, AZ: Hexagon Press, 2001.

McClanahan, Jerry. *EZ66 Guide for Travelers*. Lake Arrowhead, CA: National Historic Route 66 Federation, 2005.

Piotrowski, Scott R. *Finding the End of the Mother Road: Route 66 in Los Angeles County*. Pasadena, CA: 66 Productions, 2005 (Revised Second Printing).

Ross, Jim. *Oklahoma Route 66*. Arcadia, OK: Ghost Town Press, 2001.

Elmer McCurdy

For more on the truly bizarre tale of Oklahoma outlaw Elmer McCurdy:

Svenvold, Mark. *Elmer McCurdy: The Misadventures in Life and Afterlife of an American Outlaw*. New York: Basic Books, 2002.

National Road

For a detailed, scholarly description of the National Road/U.S. 40 as it exists today, including photographs and maps:

Raitz, Karl, ed. *A Guide to the National Road*. Baltimore, MD: The Johns Hopkins University Press, 1996.

Route 66 **the Television Series**
For a synopsis of each and every episode ever aired of the 1960s television series, as well as background information on the players, producers, etc.:

Rosin, James. *"Route 66": The Television Series, 1960–1964*. Philadelphia, PA: The Autumn Road Company, 2007.

World's Largest Catsup Bottle
Official website: www.catsupbottle.com

PHOTO CREDITS
All other photographs and illustrations © the author.

Amboy Crater: Postcard, author's collection.

Chicken Boy: www.chickenboy.com.

Chicken-in-the-Rough: Detail from advertising postcard, author's collection.

Civilian Conservation Corps: Royalty-free graphic collection.

Gay Parita: Photo courtesy of Steve Turner.

Cloverleaf: Royalty-free graphic collection.

Club Café: Menu cover, author's collection.

Coral Court Motel: Found photo, author's collection.

Dinosaur Caverns: Composite of two vintage road map details, author's collection.

Harvey House: Detail from reverse of postcard, author's collection.

Hooker Cut: Vintage postcard, author's collection.

John Steinbeck Award: Souvenir award program, author's collection.

Lincoln Highway: Cigar band, author's collection.

Meteor Crater: Postcard, author's collection.

Petrified Forest: Postcard album cover, author's collection.

Phillips 66: Logos from royalty-free graphic collection.

Route 66: Royalty-free graphic collection.

Standard Addition: Catalog cover, author's collection.

Switchback: Postcard, author's collection.

Tri-County Truck Stop: Top half of the composite, author's collection.

Robert Waldmire: Detail from postcard (used with the artist's permission).

Will Rogers Highway: Vintage map cover, author's collection.